Goodbye to Excellence

Also of Interest

The Politics of Language: The Dilemma of Bilingual Education for Puerto Ricans, Pastora San Juan Cafferty and Carmen Rivera-Martinez

*Legal Handbook for Educators, Patricia A. Hollander

*Evaluating Teachers and Administrators: A Performance Objectives Approach, George B. Redfern

*The Transition of Youth to Adulthood: A Bridge Too Long; A Report to Educators, Sociologists, Legislators, and Youth Policymaking Bodies, The National Commission on Youth

Found: Long-Term Gains from Early Intervention, edited by Bernard Brown

*Available in hardcover and paperback.

NAESP Studies in Education and Public Policy
Paul L. Houts and Sally Banks Zakariya,
Series Editors

Goodbye to Excellence:
A Critical Look at Minimum Competency Testing
Mitchell Lazarus

In recent years, concern over high school graduates who could not balance checkbooks or read directions has led many states to require students to pass minimum competency tests before receiving their diplomas. This, legislators believe, will again make diplomas meaningful, as well as promote better education. Dr. Lazarus points out that any testing scheme creates inequities and that these tests are of special concern due to the emphasis society places on high school graduation; a just society cannot accept their potential to mark a student for life.

The problem, he believes, is that society cannot agree on the goals of education, making relevant testing difficult. He also questions whether such testing will produce better curricula and notes that, while more emphasis on the basics may be needed, undue stress on them may weaken other parts of the curricula. He concludes that the goals of minimum competency testing are laudable, but that implementation may do long-term damage to education.

Mitchell Lazarus earned a master's degree in electrical engineering and a doctorate in psychology at the Massachusetts Institute of Technology while on its teaching staff. He spent six years working at the Education Development Center in educational television, mathematics curriculum, and testing and is now a consultant in the Washington, D.C., area. He has published many articles on math education, math anxiety, and testing.

Goodbye to Excellence

A Critical Look at
Minimum Competency Testing

Mitchell Lazarus

Westview Press / Boulder, Colorado

Copyright © 1981 by National Association of Elementary School Principals

Published in 1981 in the United States of America by
    Westview Press, Inc.
    5500 Central Avenue
    Boulder, Colorado 80301
    Frederick A. Praeger, Publisher

Library of Congress Cataloging in Publication Data
Lazarus, Mitchell
    Goodbye to excellence.
    (NAESP studies in education and public policy)
(Westview special studies in education)
    Bibliography: p.
    Includes index.
    1. Competency-based educational tests. I. Title. II. Series. III. Series:
Westview special studies in education.
LC1034.L39   371.2'6   81-1797
ISBN 0-89158-771-3   AACR2
ISBN 0-89158-897-3 (pbk.)

Printed and bound in the United States of America

You might as well fall flat on your face as lean over too far backward.

James Thurber

Contents

Foreword

This volume is the first in the National Association of Elementary School Principals' series "Studies in Education and Public Policy." The series will address the growing number of issues that arise where educational concerns encounter trends and developments elsewhere in an increasingly interrelated society.

It is hardly news that what happens in the schools affects, and is affected by, events beyond the schoolyard fence. We sometimes forget, though, how recently this interaction came about. Just a century ago, events in the public schools — and even in the great universities — had little to do with most people's daily lives. The schools operated in isolation, for the most part. A refuge from the physical labor of farm and factory, they marched to the drum of their own traditions.

Today, the boundaries of education are blurred and indistinct. Little belongs exclusively to the schools, and little lies entirely outside their concerns. Practically every "movement" that appears in society nowadays tries to impress itself on the curriculum, while, at the same time, school people seek to build on the education that takes place in the home, before the television set, and on the street. Moreover, from Congress and the federal agencies down to the smallest township, the politics of education have become inextricably tangled in the larger machinery of government.

This series of books will attempt to plot a course around the broad and marshy coasts of education. Taking into account both the responsibilities that educators draw from their traditional role and the new mandates that society imposes on the schools, a number of distinguished authors will bring into focus various questions of policy and practice. We are proud to launch the series with Dr. Lazarus's careful analysis of the impact that minimum competency testing will have on society at large and of its foundation in issues that relate to education only peripherally. He has set a high standard for the rest of the series, a combination of scholarship and clear thinking that, we trust, will also mark the books to follow.

Paul L. Houts and Sally Banks Zakariya
Series Editors
NAESP Studies in Education and Public Policy

Preface

To begin with, the book wasn't my idea. Credit goes to Paul L. Houts, who edits *Principal* magazine for the National Association of Elementary School Principals (NAESP).

Among educational publications, Houts's magazine stands out. Some others have the visual appeal of a World War II radar manual and read about the same way. But *Principal* has a glossy look, contains fine graphics, and presents some of the best writing in the business. The praise is not wholly gratuitous, as I write for the magazine myself, once in a while; but the company is always good.

Houts and I began to collaborate in 1975, when I wrote a couple of pieces on testing for the magazine; these later appeared in Houts's book, *The Myth of Measurability* (New York: Hart, 1977), and we also worked on a few grant proposals together. Four years later, in January 1979, he published a special issue called "Down and Out in the Classroom: Surviving Minimum Competency." It was the best collection on competency testing at the time. There was the usual talk of a book, and eventually NAESP signed a contract with Westview Press. In the meantime, the competency situation had changed so quickly that just revising the magazine issue would not be enough. Houts needed an author.

Around that time I came to see him on other business. Somebody had pirated a piece I wrote earlier for Houts—and worse, she had omitted the best part. Our conversation drifted from that to competency testing, and to what a new book might say about it, and finally to when I could start writing. As often happens in talks with Houts, we soon reached full agreement on a great many issues without saying much about any of them.

Let it be on the record that Houts gave me a completely free hand and asked for no changes in the manuscript. But he did offer a lot of excellent advice throughout. Whatever qualities the book may have are a result in large measure of his ideas and influence.

A lot of the credit also goes to Sally Banks Zakariya, senior editor of *Principal,* whose sharp pencil and keen ear for the language made my writing look better than it has any right to. Ms. Zakariya was also invaluable in locating and interpreting source materials and in many other ways helped see the work through to a conclusion.

Rita Brown typed the manuscript—some parts of it many times—with patience and skill. She has my enthusiastic appreciation.

I owe a special debt to Jerrold R. Zacharias, who shaped my thinking on testing—and excellence, for that matter—as he did in a dozen other fields. The several quotations that the book attributes to him do not begin to reflect his influence on it, and I earnestly hope that the result meets with his approval.

Special appreciation is also due the Institute for Development of Educational Activities, an affiliate of the Charles F. Kettering Foundation, for its cosponsorship with NAESP, not only of the book itself but of the 1978 conference on minimum competency testing on which *Principal*'s special issue was based.

In addition, a great many people helped through mail and over the phone, too many to list all by name. Those whose contributions stand out most in the final product include Chris Pipho and Merle McClung, both at Education Commission of the States; Diana Pullin, Center for Law and Education; Robert B. Burns, University of California at Santa Barbara; the people at American College Testing Program; Anne Lewis and Holly DiVenere of *Education USA,* National School Public Relations Association; Alan Dyson and John Cawthorne of Education Development Center's Project TORQUE; Walt Haney at the Huron Institute, which acts as the research staff for the National Consortium on Testing; Kay Watson, National Consortium on Testing (who also compiled the list of references for this book); and a marvelously helpful woman (whose name I don't know) at Educational Research Service. I appreciate Lystra Blake's careful work in checking the legal citations. In places the book draws heavily on the views of several authors who contributed to "Down and Out in the Classroom: Surviving Minimum Competency"; to them I am indebted accordingly. None of these people, however, are in any way responsible for errors, omissions, or misrepresentations. Those are solely my doing.

I am also grateful to the library staffs at Georgetown University Law Center and the George Mason University School of Law. And a special word of apology to my young children, Margaret and Ben, on whose activities the writing too often infringed.

It goes without saying that the pronoun "he" always means "he or she" where appropriate. Including a full set of pronouns for each use would have made for heavy going here and there, so I opted for consistency with the short form in most places. I trust that readers of both sexes will appreciate the problem.

The hybrid system of citation needs a word of explanation. Two kinds of sources were used, both in substantial numbers: (1) scholarly books and papers, and (2) legal decisions and law review articles. The two customarily require very different citation forms. I have used both forms when appropriate. Scholarly materials are noted in text by author and date, and complete citations are listed at the end of the text. Legal materials are cited by superscript numerals, which correspond to the numbered notes collected at the end of each chapter. Many of these notes also contain explanatory discussions.

Mitchell Lazarus

1

Why Minimum Competency Testing?

There is currently a conviction in the land that the schools are not as good as they used to be. In truth, they probably never were as good as we remember them to be. Most of us cannot help using our own school days as the yardstick, try though we may to be objective. But memory makes a cloudy lens, conveying its images in a warm, hazy glow that obscures blemishes of the past. And recollections from childhood have a special liability toward improvement over the years.

The sense of declining education also seems to be supported by more objective evidence. Test scores have fallen over the past fifteen years. Employers complain that high school graduates are less prepared than before to take their places in the economy. The military has similar problems in filling its needs. Colleges and universities find that incoming freshmen are unready for college studies. Well-publicized lawsuits have documented graduating students who can neither read nor write. Millions of parents are dissatisfied with the slight academic demands made on their school-age children. And daily, the newspapers report occasions of violence, vandalism, and drug use in the nation's schools.

We shall have to dip an oar of our own into these murky waters. For the moment, though, it is enough to ask whether comparisons between past and present are truly valid at all. Social conditions have been changing continually. There are marked differences in the student body of every generation—especially evident today, when students who once would have been allowed to drop out quietly are now the target of an intense campaign to keep them in school. Even the broad goals of education have undergone substantial shifts in just the past few decades.

In the face of all these changes, it is very difficult to determine whether the apparent declines in education are real and, if so, whether the schools are responsible. Even if the schools were known to be at fault, that information still would not tell us what they are doing wrong. There are plenty of theories on this question; ask anyone. But the theories all rest more or less on guesswork, because no one has found a way to evaluate the issues with good evidence.

Minimum competency testing is an effort to solve certain problems in education without first understanding what the problems are. In medical terms, minimum competency testing amounts to treating the symptom without paying much attention to the underlying ailment. Here the major symptom is a number of high school graduates who cannot read, write, and figure well enough to function adequately in society. No one knows how many there are, though they certainly constitute a small fraction of all high school graduates. The treatment for this symptom? Test all students in the basic skills of reading, writing, and arithmetic. Some states go further; they make receipt of a high school diploma conditional on the student's passing the test.

Whether such a diploma sanction applies or not, minimum competency testing is precisely what the name implies: a program to test students in terms of, and only in terms of, whatever competencies state or local authorities have decided are the minimally acceptable result of an education.

Minimum competency testing is not the same thing as competency-based education (CBE), though the two are easy to confuse. They do have certain goals in common and, adding to the confusion, CBE often includes minimum competency tests as one of its components. CBE is a much broader and more complex enterprise. It directly affects the instructional process; but competency testing, in principle at least, is confined to measuring certain outcomes of instruction.

CBE attempts to set clearly defined objectives for all levels of education. The objectives typically reflect a strong focus on basic skills. It is part of the CBE philosophy that objectives be set by educators and the community, so that objectives reflect a realistic appraisal of the skills that students will actually need after they leave school.

Most CBE classroom instruction is designed specifically to suit these objectives, is organized around them, and follows them closely in all respects. A student's progress is assessed primarily in terms of the objectives he has mastered. The goals in CBE are typically more ambitious and less minimal than those specified for competency testing. But in many districts that use CBE, students must also pass a competency exam before graduation. Other districts ask that students master a minimal core of CBE objectives, again as reflected in test results. CBE tends to take on different forms wherever it has been adopted. As a general rule, though, CBE calls for a fundamental restructuring of curriculum and teaching (National School Public Relations Association 1978).

Minimum competency testing, though it professes much more limited goals, also varies markedly among states. There have been proposals for a uniform federal standard, but neither the Congress nor the executive agencies have shown much interest. No doubt the state governments would resent federal intrusion, as education is historically and constitutionally a state enterprise. In the meantime, though, the diversity of programs makes it difficult to generalize beyond the borders of a particular state. A book such as this one, which attempts to look at the situation nationally, must sometimes fall back on generalizations that do not apply in every jurisdiction.

Pipho (1979*b*) supplies detailed information on the individual states. From more recent data, which Pipho very kindly provided me with, I count 38 states that have mandated competency tests in the basic skills. Sixteen of them flatly require students to pass the test in order to receive their diplomas, a requirement either in effect now or to become effective at a specified date in the future. These "diploma states" include some of the most populous, particularly California and New York. In what amounts to a similar practice, New Mexico endorses the diplomas of only those who pass the competency test. Colorado and New Hampshire leave the diploma sanction up to the local districts. So does Idaho; but there, students from participating districts who pass the test receive a special state seal on their diplomas.

Thus, in one way or another, a total of 20 states link passing the test to graduation. Kentucky also had planned to, but changed its mind. Maine gave its test only once, in order to gather data for a policy study. Kansas has just completed a two-year pilot study. Of the remaining 15 competency states, a few expressly rule out a diploma sanction, and the rest do not mention it either way. All of the states with no competency program have such a program under legislative consideration (Beckham 1980).

About half of the state competency programs were put into effect by the state legislatures and the other half by the state departments of education (Gorth and Perkins 1979). But in practice it makes little difference which body was the moving force. If the legislature disapproves of a department-initiated competency program, it can always overrule the program. The competency program in every state can be assumed to have its legislature's endorsement, either active or passive. And in some states, it is likely that the department acted first in order to head off legislative intervention. Thus, when I speak elsewhere of a competency program deriving from the legislature, I also include other state-level bodies with the legislature's tacit accord.

To students, the most important single question is whether their own state requires them to pass the test in order to graduate. As we have seen, the states vary in this respect. Some parts of this book are concerned primarily with the diploma sanction, for example, where I discuss the effects of minimum competency testing on minority and handicapped students. However, it should always be clear from the context whether a discussion applies only to the diploma states or instead to all of the states with minimum competency programs.

Most of the 38 competency states, even those with a diploma sanction, use the tests for other purposes as well. Several states give a preliminary test in grade eight or nine, and many others begin testing systematically in elementary school. Some states require passing scores for promotion from certain grades. In most states, students who early show signs of trouble are identified as candidates for remediation, in the hope that special attention will improve their chances of passing.

Averaging the test scores can also show whether students are doing better or worse over time in particular skills. Thus, the tests might be used to judge educational programs. Although no legislation that I know of mentions this, the test results would also make it easy for state agencies to compare the performance of individual districts or for districts to monitor the performance of individual schools and perhaps even specific teachers. All such evaluations, of course, would be limited to the particular content of the tests.

The states also vary among themselves in how much discretion they leave to local school districts. In Michigan, for example, the state develops and administers the tests but turns the results over to local districts to use as they see fit. Utah requires that students pass a test to graduate, but lets its local districts choose both the tests and the passing scores. Next door in Nevada, the state both selects the test and sets the standards.

There are wide discrepancies in the skills tested. All of the minimum competency states evaluate reading, and most test writing and arithmetic as well, though Colorado leaves these, too, up to its local districts. A few states require a knowledge of government and there is a scattering of other topics.

The states disagree further on whether to examine school skills or "life skills." Moreover, there are two kinds of life skills, fundamentally different for testing purposes but often confused. One approach is to dress up a school skill so as to resemble a problem that the student might encounter in real life. For example, multiplying numbers in the abstract is a school skill; multiplying the same numbers to figure a sales tax is a life skill. Despite a noisy debate on which of these skills is the more appropriate to evaluate, the skills do not look much different when reduced to test form.

The other kind of life skill involves knowledge beyond the three Rs that people need (presumably) to cope with daily problems in society. Test items of this type deal with health and nutrition information, consumers' rights, employees' rights, etc. There is a special difficulty with these items, because a student's view of which answer is correct may depend partly on local conditions and personal experience. Later in this chapter, we shall look at some examples of how different answers might look correct to different students.

For the most part, test items take the familiar form of multiple choice, and for familiar reasons: economy in scoring by machine and the claim of objectivity and consistency in scoring. I shall examine this second claim in some detail in the following chapter.

Effects of Minimum Competency Testing

Minimum competency testing has spread around the country with stunning speed. Educators are accustomed to sweeping changes overnight; they could easily put "new math" into every classroom in a couple of years and a decade later, would need only a couple of years to take it out again. But many competency testing programs were started by state legislatures, bodies not often given to swift and consistent action. It is remarkable to see so many states passing laws, which have at least some resemblance to one another, at a rate of several states per year. The usual approach is for a state to watch other states struggle for a few years before passing its own laws, in the hope of learning from their mistakes. Competency testing must appear to hold special promise for so many states to climb on board so fast.

What is that promise? Exactly what do the states and districts hope to accomplish through their testing programs? Again, the answers vary from state to state. In very general terms, these are the goals that a majority of the states have mentioned or implied:

1. To make the diploma meaningful by ensuring that people who carry it have at least the minimum ability to read, write, and compute—meaningful only in those states that have diploma sanctions, of course;

2. To help employers identify (through the diploma) job candidates who have these minimum skills;

3. To pressure students to acquire the minimum skills, and thus become more employable, better able to act as informed consumers, and better equipped for a satisfying life;

4. To pressure schools and teachers to provide more instruction in the basics, less in "frills";

5. To identify students who need remediation in the basic skills;

6. To create a consistent data base for monitoring the progress of education on a statewide basis.

Some less charitable motives have also been ascribed to the states adopting minimum competency programs:

7. To respond to political pressure to "do something" about the schools — as quickly and inexpensively as possible;

8. To strengthen state influence over local education;

9. To support a management model that sees the educational system in factory terms, which requires a measurement of output;

10. To resegregate society by denying diplomas, and hence employment, to substantial numbers of minority youth while certifying the large majority of whites.

The competency programs in some states are having all of these effects, whether intended or not. Most items on the list, and especially the last item, will come up for discussion in subsequent chapters.

In fields other than education, it might be surprising to find a mere test having such far-reaching effects. Ordinarily we think of a test as something for measuring outcomes, not as a tool to control those outcomes. Using the testers' own jargon, a test in itself is just a "sample of behavior," or a reasonably systematic way to gather data from many people at once. A test by itself cannot effect change; it can only record whether change is taking place. One might as well expect to cool a room by putting a thermometer in it.

In education, however, tests have long had a disproportionate impact on whatever was being tested. The test results have a way of feeding back to the educational process. Most school people want test scores to be as high as possible for the sake of their own reputations and funding. As a result, there is a tendency to adopt whatever educational content and method promise good scores. The test in practice tends to act more like a thermostat than a thermometer, adjusting the mechanisms that determine its own readings.

One clear example of the tests' influence is in the way they inhibit improvement in education. To be sure, educational reformers, or at least the more sophisticated among them, have long realized that tests offer excellent leverage over most of educational practice. Almost any innovation that might raise test scores has an excellent chance of catching on. Before minimum competency testing, some reformers tried to exploit this effect by seeking changes in the most widely used achievement tests — changes that would make the tests more responsive to whatever educational improvements the reformers sought and thus make the improvements that much more attractive to the schools.

Virtually all of the achievement tests in common use, however, are produced by the same half-dozen companies. Most of these companies are divisions of textbook publishers — though the biggest, the non-profit Educational Testing Service (ETS), is a separate operation. Some of these same firms, including ETS, now also handle competency testing for several states.

The companies nearly always resist suggested changes in their achievement tests, regardless of pedagogical value. Senior officials of one large testing firm I spoke with were quite candid about why. A test on the market represents a large investment in development. The only way to recover that investment is to sell many copies of the test. And not only is a new test an expensive proposition in itself, but the market for any new test is chancy — especially when such a test reflects a change in educational practice. The company is betting, in effect, that the educational innovation will take hold and then persist at least long enough for recovery of the investment. (Testmakers still do not like to talk about the "new math," which came and went in less than ten years.) Any changes in the product line represent a substantial financial risk for the company. This may be especially true in terms of changing tests for basic skills like reading and arithmetic, where the industry finds a large share of its market.

Tests thus impede nearly all attempts at educational reform, due to a combination of two factors: the importance that school people attach to the scores and the difficulty of promoting change in the tests. The companies prefer to cast their role in positive terms, speaking of it as a "stabilizing influence" on education. (Jerrold Zacharias, one of the few innovators to bring about major changes in the Scholastic Aptitude Test, once called the testers' role a "stranglehold" instead.)

Whether the influence of tests is a help or a hindrance to education, there is no denying that the quest for high scores gives the tests a great deal of control over what the schools teach and how they teach it. On another occasion, speaking prior to minimum competency testing, Zacharias described the testing industry's relationship to the rest of education as a "$10 million tail wagging a $100 billion dog." By the time the states felt a need to strengthen the teaching of basic skills, this history was already well established. It helps to explain why so many states chose to institute tests that measure educational outcomes instead of acting on the educational process more directly.

A state government or education department can mandate almost any changes in schooling that it wishes to. For example, a state can impose a specific curriculum, control textbook selection, oversee the selection of teachers, and even allocate so many hours a day to any particular subject. Some of these options might run afoul of the local districts politically; but the options are still within the state's power to implement.

A test, however, is a particularly efficient means of exerting control over curriculum, textbooks, and all other educational practices. If the old tests kept education from changing, then a new test can just as easily require it to change. The states, unlike mere individuals and groups who want to change education, do not have the problem of convincing test publishers that the changes they want will find a sufficient market. The state government simply has to require the new test by law and ap-

propriate the funds to pay for it. This assures both ample
development money and a captive market—a testing company's
dream.

Representatives of the test publishers lobbied in state
legislatures to make sure that minimum competency test laws
passed. There was little talk then of tests as a "stabilizing influence"; with profitable contracts just around the corner, tests
had suddenly become the ideal vehicle for educational change.
And once the laws were enacted, the testing companies scram-
bled to convince state officials that private enterprise was best
equipped to develop the tests, administer and score them, and
collect the money. Though organized under the tax laws as a
nonprofit corporation, the Educational Testing Service did its
part to further the competency testing movement and collected
its share of the contracts.

There still remains, though, the question of why states preferred to implement the changes they wanted with tests rather
than working on the educational mechanism itself. The goal,
after all, is not test scores as such, but young people who can
read and write. Why settle for a thermometer, or even a thermostat, when the full set of controls to the air conditioner is in
easy reach? Besides, there is always the possibility—a very real
possibility, we shall see—that even good test scores may not indicate student literacy, and vice versa. Despite some carefully
worded arguments to the contrary, the main motives for requiring a test do not seem to be grounded in pedagogical concerns at
all. Rather, they seem to rest on the more pragmatic questions
of politics, management, and money.

Political Basis of Minimum Competency Testing

The political environment surrounding education has lately
become quite delicate. In a tradition dating back to colonial
times, education in the United States has been viewed as a local
concern, under the control of locally elected or appointed
school boards. Some other nations, in contrast, govern education rigidly from the top, with every important decision being
made at what we would call the federal level. At least since
World War II, however, the United States has been moving

toward more central administrative structures. One factor is that the money for education comes increasingly from the state and federal governments, less from local property taxes. It rarely comes unencumbered. And even before minimum competency testing, the state legislatures had taken substantial amounts of control away from local authorities by passing assorted legislation on a wide variety of topics. The federal government does not prescribe educational policy as such, having no authority under the Constitution to do so. But it does attach very detailed regulations to the federal money on which both states and local school districts have come to depend. Along with this steady erosion of local control, of course, have come fine speeches about its continuing vitality.

The courts, too, at both the state and federal levels, exert a great deal of control over some aspects of local policies and procedure. By far the best examples of court control are the busing decisions. But the courts have gone against local and state wishes in many other matters, including compulsory education, censorship of library materials, regulation of students' hairstyles and dress, disciplinary procedures, teacher terminations, students' political expression, etc.

In the face of legislative action particularly, local jurisdictions see government actions as heavy-handed interference. Every locality is proud of its uniqueness; each resents becoming a nameless cog in some large plan. The complaint of school boards nationwide is that "the people in Albany [or Sacramento or Washington] just don't understand what we're up against here!"

Being sensitive to this tension between state and local prerogatives and reluctant to exacerbate it more than necessary, a state legislature would find it awkward to impose specific educational practices directly. But a test is easy to defend politically. The state can take the position that it merely wants to monitor students' progress in the basic skills, which is certainly within its mandate. The legislature can even make the districts responsible for having their students achieve a certain minimum score on the test, without incurring much objection. As long as the state leaves the means for doing so to local authorities, the principle of local control remains ostensibly intact. Yet as a practical matter, the test itself will change the face of education throughout the state, down to the last detail. The test takes a large bite out of local control, but it does so inconspicuously.

Moreover, legislators like to keep their constituents happy and voting "properly." Through the late 1960s and early 1970s, the public became increasingly disaffected with the educational system. In many places the reported declines in basic skills became an issue in both state and local elections. The legislatures came under increasing pressure to repair what many voters saw as a major problem. But when the legislatures turned to their appointed school people, solutions were not forthcoming. Some educators denied that a decline had taken place at all and brought out suitcases full of statistics to prove it. Others conceded a decline but blamed it on factors outside the schools' control, especially television and changes in student demographics. (The latter most often translated to more black or Hispanic children.) Some educators agreed that improvement was necessary but admitted that they had not the slightest idea of what the underlying problems were or of how to go about fixing them. All of these groups unanimously agreed, however, that more money for the schools would certainly help.

Because the only consistent answer they heard was a call for more funds, the legislatures tried to raise them. But voters began turning down school bond issues with depressing regularity. According to the public opinion polls, voters did so as an expression of protest, in essence refusing to spend good money after bad. Yet the same voters wanted improvement, and they wanted to see it immediately.

Requiring a test was an ideal solution to this political dilemma, regardless of whether it would really help in the long run—or even in the short run, for that matter. Testing is relatively cheap compared to other forms of intervention. It is highly conspicuous; newspapers everywhere have given wide coverage to competency test programs and especially enjoy printing test results. (In Florida, educational authorities even prepared a mock-up version of the test for reporters to take. The resulting publicity was enormous. The news people all passed the English portion easily, but a few had real trouble with the math.) A test can be instituted quickly, in a matter of a year or so, thus satisfying the demand for immediate action. And the test itself can easily be constructed around whatever content seems to most concern the public, usually just the three Rs.

The installation of a test thus handles most of the political problems quite nicely. The test can also get rid of another problem—the charge that too many high school graduates cannot read or write—with a simple requirement. The solution is to graduate only those students who *can* read and write. The rest of the students, those who put in 12 years and leave school with a certificate of incompetence, are mostly poor and from minority groups and thus not of great political concern. This solution misses the real problem of illiteracy, of course, but it does cover the problem with a lot of reassuring talk about high standards.

Educational reform through testing also appeals to a particular philosophy of educational management. Raymond E. Callahan (1962) has written on the conflicts in management style that have attended education since the turn of the century. On the one hand, educators have traditionally seen themselves in the same professional caste as physicians, attorneys, and clergymen, as a guiding force in shaping the nation's future through the enlightenment of its young minds. But at the same time, the schools are large and complicated enterprises. They consume a great deal of money and are expected to produce certain outcomes in return—in some respects, much like a commercial operation. Accordingly, there has sometimes been a tendency to operate the schools in accordance with industrial practices. This puts the emphasis on efficiency, or, in the more current phrase, cost-effectiveness. The relative popularity of these two styles, the intellectual and the industrial, has shifted back and forth over the decades.

In recent times, for example, we saw a regrowth of professionalism in the 1960s. Its most visible sign was the high schools modeling themselves after the colleges. The teaching staff restyled itself a faculty. The system of required courses and electives came to resemble that most often associated with the colleges. Even college-level courses became commonplace in the high schools. Many of the changes were superficial, but they reflected an attitude that ran deeper—a sense that education is important for its own sake, that a society is a better place when citizens have insight and wisdom. Teachers in those days could talk about academic values without embarrassment. The high schools saw themselves, proudly, as a link in the great pedagogical tradition that goes back to Socrates teaching in the marketplace.

The 1970s changed much of that. Resources shrank; public dissatisfaction grew. This combination triggered a "back to basics" movement that swept the country in just a year or two. The loftier goals of a decade earlier were largely forgotten. Every program came in for close scrutiny. Suddenly, all that mattered was results—and results always meant better scores on the achievement tests. Principals studied their percentile averages with the same anxiety that television producers bring to the Nielsen ratings. To borrow an unfortunate phrase from the Pentagon, educators began seeking "more bang for the buck."

In the end, administrators came to view the school as a mass-production plant. One educator, writing with an apparently straight face, recently referred to a school as a "learning delivery system." Another, advocating a particular curriculum reform, boasted that it brought a "businesslike atmosphere" to the classroom. Children have become raw materials; instruction is the analogue to manufacture; and the main product is test scores. Any other benefits to the child seem to be mostly a by-product. Even the sociologists, the scientists who should be most concerned with the human values involved, have fallen into line. At least one very influential study, Christopher Jencks' *Inequality* (1972), unabashedly used a factory model of the school—dollars in, test scores out—to question the value of education in improving people's fortunes (Lazarus 1977*b*).

By the mid-1970s, when most states had either passed minimum competency legislation or had it under active consideration, this nuts-and-bolts approach to educational management was already secure. Its needs and priorities were important in helping to make minimum competency testing attractive. The test promised to handle a key step in what manufacturers call quality control—in this case, the final inspection before the goods are shipped. Moreover, industrial management requires good data from intermediate stages of production if it is to achieve the best possible allocation of resources. The proposal to test students at several points during their school careers helped to fill this need as well. In addition, all the data would come from consistently administered tests over whose content the state educators had full control. Minimum competency testing fit ideally into the industrial management environment.

Competency programs also make it more likely that the industrial style of school management will continue to prevail in the future. In effect, the legislation acts to set attainment of the minimum competencies as a social goal, and it also invites public attention to the test scores. Thus, the most important indicator of a school's success has become the proportion of its students who can display the required competencies on the test. Stretching the industrial analogy a little, it is as if a firm that had traditionally turned out individually handmade items, all of them different, decided to standardize its product and make as many as possible. An emphasis on quantity of output inevitably impairs the quality of the product — and so it is with the schools. The move toward quantity in the schools also invites the kind of management best suited to quantity output of a uniform product, with the accompanying emphasis on results and cost-effectiveness.

Unless the minimum competency statutes are repealed, educators have every political reason to continue running the schools like factories. Repeal has been proposed in some states, but a national movement in that direction is still many years away. In the meantime, we are likely to continue seeing educational programs evaluated primarily in terms of their effects on minimum competency scores. Academic values will have to stay very much in the background for several years to come.

There are still educators everywhere who persist in seeing their students as people with individual potential, who seek to inspire in their students a love of learning for its own sake. There are many more educators who claim to do so — who point to minor variations in their local programs as evidence that education in the traditional sense is still their goal — but whose work from day to day must cast doubts on their sincerity. Despite the efforts of the few for whom the ancient calling of teaching is a source of pride, the quest for excellence in our schools has largely given way to a scramble for test scores. Indeed, the law all but requires it.

Several critics of competency testing have complained in print that the scheme is not only harmful to education but costly as well. But that depends on one's viewpoint. I must note that the estimates of actual costs range so widely as to be hardly worth reproducing here—typically from around one dollar to several tens of dollars per student. Much of the discrepancy, no doubt, is because different estimates include different cost items (Anderson 1977). Any estimate would have to include the cost of printing and scoring the test. But some may not account for planning, developing, and validating the test; staff expenses in test administration; the costs of handling, computing, and reporting scores; the expense of revising the test when necessary; and especially the costs of remedial instruction for students who fail—the biggest item of all.

It is easy to prove that the testing process is expensive. A state close to the national mean has about 850,000 students enrolled (Dearman and Plisko 1980). If the state tests in four grades, it will test a third of its students each year, or almost 300,000 students. Arbitrarily taking a cost of $10 per student tested, that works out to nearly $3 million per year for testing alone—or enough to hire almost 200 more teachers. This cost is for a state roughly the size of Tennessee or Louisiana; the costs would be much higher in a big state like California or New York.

But it is also easy to prove that the cost of testing is negligible, at least on a relative basis. Testing one student four times, still at our arbitrary guess of $10 each time, amounts to $40. Now, compare that to the total cost of educating the same student. My own projection from the most recent data available to me (Dearman and Plisko 1980) shows that we now spend about $1,600 per pupil per year, averaged nationally. Over 12 years of schooling, this would come to $19,200. Still, a student graduating in 1980, say, will have incurred much of the cost of his education at a lower rate, due to rising costs while he was in school. Making a generous allowance for this inflation, we might estimate the total cost of his education to be something like $12,000.

The cost of $40 to test that same student is miniscule in comparison to his other educational costs. In some states, the fruit of his education—in the form of a diploma—depends solely on how well he performs on the test. The expense of testing turns out to be hardly worth mention in relation to the larger figures. The cost factor is, or ought to be, a minor consideration in evaluations of minimum competency testing. In all fairness, the cost of minimum competency testing simply does not make that much difference to the total cost of education.

One cost element that is *not* negligible, however, is that of providing remediation for students who fail the test. However, the state can control this expense. At any time, it can reduce the number of students involved by simply adjusting the cutoff scores so that fewer fail. Many considerations go into choosing a cutoff, and this may often be one of them.

Even so, educators in some states have complained that their legislature mandated testing and also remediation for failing students but appropriated money only for the testing process. School people in such states face a considerable added burden in extra instruction with no way to pay for it. In the end, the money must come out of the programs for students who already perform well enough on the test not to require remediation.

Even in states that do allocate money expressly for remediation, the funds to support it must come from some larger pool of resources. In many cases, the cost of remediation will simply reduce the support that otherwise would have been available for other educational activities. This is one of the ways in which competency testing can work to the detriment of better students. We shall come to others later in the book.

Are the Tests Good Enough?

In terms of politics and management, minimum competency tests do solve certain short-term problems for school administrators, and, except for the matter of remediation, they do so at little cost. But what is the effect on students? Proponents argue that students gain from competency testing. A student who passes the test has a more valuable diploma—in states that tie the diploma to the test—because it certifies his or her mastery of the minimum skills. And those who fail are helped as well, because the test identifies them as candidates for the remediation that they need.

These arguments presuppose, however, that the test is a good indicator of the competencies tested. If it is not — if the test fails any students who should pass or passes some who should fail — then the process is harmful to those who are misjudged. The result is that capable students are wrongly identified as illiterate. And some students who need remediation will receive only a handshake from the principal instead.

There is reason to doubt that a test like those typically used for minimum competency can divide the skilled from the not-yet-skilled without considerable error. The problem is not with these tests in particular but with tests of school achievement generally. The art of testing is not yet sufficiently advanced to meet the demands that minimum competency places on it.

As a group, educators put a lot of faith in test scores — often more than the test makers themselves would. Reputable test publishers give warnings in their manuals about possible margins of error, and they specify the populations for whom the test is intended. Yet school people often ignore these limitations (if they read about them at all) and wrongly regard every child's score as precise and highly accurate.[1] Sometimes educators make decisions based not on student ability but on score differences that are so fine as to reflect mostly test error.

The testing companies use an involved process to write questions, try them out, and decide which questions to use in the final versions of the test. When the process is carried through properly, the result is a test that separates students into categories — though always with some error and not necessarily into the categories that the test giver wants. Furthermore, the most important parts of the development procedure do not study the questions themselves with any care. Instead, the procedure focuses mostly on statistical tallies of which students answered which questions correctly. It is very common for defective questions to slip through, usually questions that are either ambiguous or have right answers counted as wrong. There is a surprising number of such questions in even the most widely used tests. The publisher's usual defense is that such questions produce the same statistical patterns as questions without apparent defects. But it is hard to believe that students are never misled, that they always answer defective questions the same as they do good ones. Though some in the testing industry might disagree, it seems evident that a test can be no better than the questions it consists of.

The educational community had fair warning about tests in use almost a generation ago with the publication of Banesh Hoffmann's excellent book *The Tyranny of Testing* (1962). Hoffmann explored in detail how tests can, and often do, misrepresent students' abilities. He included dozens of defective questions from actual tests. For some of these questions, he included and discussed the publishers' attempts to defend them. The thrust of his book, if I may high-handedly compress it to a sentence, is that test scores are not worthy of our trust.

One might have expected that Hoffmann's arguments, based on evidence he provides in the book itself, would have caused a wave of test-wariness among educators. Curiously though, and despite Hoffmann's long-standing reputation as a careful and thorough scholar, the book was largely ignored in the schools. The use of tests continued to expand in the two decades following its publication, and tests also came to serve purposes they had not served before.

The book is still worth careful study. The test questions have changed over the years, but the kinds of defects Hoffmann points out continue to recur. Here, however, although a few questions will appear by way of example, I shall be more concerned with the limitations basic to the testing mechanism.

Every test is subject to inherent error.[2] A student takes a test and receives a score, but that score always has a known probability of being wrong, for that student, by a certain number of points. Thus in practice the student's "true score" can never be determined. His or her score on the test is only an estimate of the true score. The better the test, the closer to the true score the estimate is likely to be. But even on the best tests, the range of error can be wide enough to seriously misrepresent the student's abilities. I must stress that *every* test is subject to this kind of error for every student who takes it.

The test companies should properly report, for each student, not a single score, but a range of scores in which the student's true score probably falls. One reason test companies do not report ranges is that it would require test users to think a little more about what the scores mean, which, in turn, might shake the user's faith in the test's precision. This could work against the test publishers. (Public opinion polls, incidentally, are subject to a mathematical error that is very similar to test error. A newscaster reports that public satisfaction with the president stands at 45 percent and then adds, "There is a margin of error of plus or minus 3 percentage points." He is making the report much more honest. The percentage of people satisfied is probably between 42 and 48 percent, but not necessarily 45 percent.)

What happens when we subject an error-prone test to a sharp cutoff score, as happens in a minimum competency situation? Inevitably, the result is a certain number of misclassified students. With statistical information about the test, it is even possible to calculate how many students will be misclassified—though not to say who they will be. And again, it is a mathematical certainty that some of the students will be so affected.

This is the state of affairs with a test of the very best kind—one constructed in strict accordance with industry ideals. But few minimum competency tests are that good, and many are far worse. Under the pressures of time, money, and the urge to do the work in-house, many states have produced tests whose quality is very dubious indeed. An attorney now challenging such a test in court described the test to me as "thrown together."

Some minimum competency tests are also liable to a special kind of defect that does not arise often in ordinary tests of school achievement, or even in competency tests of "school skills." The competency movement has instituted questions of a new sort—those asking for information that people might need in coping from day to day as adults. As I noted earlier, local conditions and a student's own experiences can color his responses to these questions. Indeed, almost every question of this type that I have seen has at least two defensible answers. A few instances may illustrate the point.

The examples below are paraphrased from two high school versions of the APL (Adult Performance Level) Program test distributed by the American College Testing Program. It is probably the most widely adopted test of its type; it is used throughout New Mexico and in many local districts nationwide to assess minimum competency. Each question offers four alternative answers, but two or three will suffice for our purposes. The student must choose one answer only:

- Before going to a job interview, the applicant should: contact his last employer for a letter of reference *or* ask his high school or college for a transcript *or* write down all of his past work experience. (Is the job in the mail room, or in technical work, or in sales? The question does not say—but the correct answer asks for work experience. I'm not sure why.)

- What information is NOT available on television: the cost of food at a local grocery store *or* how much a doctor charges for an operation. (In my city, food store commercials rarely quote prices, but surgery costs are sometimes a news item.)

- To read a book about car repair without buying it one should go to a: public library *or* bookstore. (Those books always seem to be checked out at my library. Personally, I find it easier to read them at the local bookstore.)

- A tenant whose apartment has a short circuit that the landlord has not fixed should notify: the fire department *or* the city housing commission. (Some cities are famous for their unresponsive housing commissions—the "correct" answer. The fire department might act more quickly to require repair of a fire hazard.)

Answering questions like these is largely an exercise in mind-reading. The student's task is to put aside what he knows and instead figure out what the test author thinks he should know. The same problem also turns up in "school skill" questions, though usually in more subtle forms.

The APL test was designed and tried out by an independent group at the University of Texas at Austin. The problems I point out may not be entirely the fault of the authors. Rather, they arise from the inescapable fact that effective coping skills must vary from place to place and from person to person. Real life is not consistent enough to permit a national test — or even a state test — on how to deal with it.

There are two ways to avoid this problem in examining life skills, both used in other questions on the APL. One solution is to make three of the answers hopelessly absurd, which renders the correct answer easy for anyone who can read the question. The other solution is to provide enough information in the question itself to rule out three of the answers. But that turns the question into one on reading or logical thinking, not on survival knowledge. In short, it is probably impossible to construct a meaningful test of "life skills" in the multiple-choice format. And, as we shall see, there are also difficulties in the testing of "school skills."

When a state develops its own test, the results are often even worse than those from a commercially produced test. Commercial tests, and independent tests like the APL, must at least cope with the demands of the marketplace. A poor test is unlikely to sell, once its quality has become known. But a state-developed test has its market established by law. The state's testing office becomes, in effect, a monopoly, but with none of the regulatory oversight that attends monopolies in other fields.

Worse, if a state-developed test is a bad one, no one is ever likely to find out about it. Tests are secret. Keeping them secret spares their makers the trouble and expense of making new versions each time the test is used. Students take the same test, or many of the same test questions, year after year. But secrecy also saves the testers from the trouble and expense of having their product criticized by outsiders. Informed criticism is all but impossible because the people who might be able to find defects in the test are denied access to it.

As a rule, only three groups of people have access to a minimum competency test: (1) the test authors and their consultants; (2) the students who take it; and (3) the typists, proof readers, printers, and others incidental to the production. None of these people is in a position to examine the test critically. The authors are presumably happy with it, as they are the ones who declared it fit for use. The students cannot keep their copies of the test and never learn which answers are counted correct. (Besides, probably no one except Hoffmann [1962, pp. 199ff.] has ever taken seriously the complaints of a disgruntled student.) And objections from the third group do not carry much weight.

This means a test can have several questions that are fatally defective—ambiguous, or just plain wrong—and there is no one who can say so. It is, to say the least, an unusual state of affairs in an open society. Apart from national defense, few important decisions are made completely outside the reach of public scrutiny. Nowadays we can even demand to see the FBI's files on our children, if they have any. And in education particularly, the trend is toward public involvement in textbook selection, hiring high officials, and even choosing teachers, in some places. But the public still cannot inspect the test on which its children's diplomas may depend.

Secrecy in testing has been the practice for decades, but it is harmful for several reasons. Mistakes concerning particular children go uncaught. Large-scale mistakes from computer errors can also be missed. A mistake in scoring the Medical College Admission Test a few years ago, which involved thousands of students, was detected barely in time (Corbett 1979), and no medical applicant can now feel fully secure in his test scores. For a time, the Law School Admissions Test was falsely identifying some students as "unacknowledged repeaters"—as people who lied in saying that they were taking the test for the first time. That mistake, too, was discovered, but only when a law school admissions officer was honest with a highly qualified student about why he had rejected her. The simple expedient of returning students' materials after scoring would eliminate most such problems. At present, there is no way of telling how common such errors are.

Making the questions and answers public would have an even more important result over the long run: It would lead to eventual improvement of the tests. For the first time, there could be an open debate on the merits of the whole business, from broad philosophies of testing to individual alternative answers. Such a debate is impossible now. The testing companies guard the security of the tests very closely. And when a leak does occur, they rely on the law to stifle criticism.

An anecdote may help to illustrate how the test companies use the law to prevent criticism. Three graduate students, already competent professionals in their field, took a certain test at the request of prospective employers. The students subsequently wrote a thoughtful article criticizing the test's approach to personnel evaluation in their field. To lend their arguments substance, they felt it necessary to reproduce three questions from the test verbatim. That, of course, would require access to a copy of the test.

The authors of the article approached Paul Houts, the editor of *Principal* magazine and a prominent figure in the current testing controversy (Houts 1977). Houts felt that the article was pertinent, as many of his readers used the results of the test in question. Accordingly, he approached the test publishers. They agreed to provide him with a copy of the test in exchange for his signing certain papers. Houts signed and received the test, whereupon the authors completed their work and submitted the finished article.

Being a fair man, Houts sent a copy of the article to the test publishers with an invitation to respond to it in print. Their answer: an attorney's letter threatening suit if the test questions were published in the article. In the paper that Houts had signed was a provision that he would not divulge the contents of the test. Yet without signing it, he could not have seen a copy of the test at all.

From a legal standpoint, the firm was probably within its rights—on the basis of possible breach of contract, though not on the basis of copyright infringement. And the firm's tactic succeeded: Houts refrained from publication because he could not expose the members of his parent association to the expense and risk of a lawsuit that could so easily be avoided. The tactic is a common one. It serves to shield the test publishers from criticism that might either advise people who use the test results or inform the public.

This is, however, a curious departure from the usual practice in a scientific or intellectual enterprise—and the testing community identifies itself with both science and scholarship. In every other field (again excepting defense-related matters), there is a centuries-old tradition of holding out work to one's peers for review and confirmation. Scientists and scholars alike vigorously guard the right to publish theories and findings, even in the face of opposition, harking proudly to Galileo's defiant *Epur si muove!* ("Nevertheless, the earth does move!").

Not in testing, though. When a bill was proposed in New York State that would require tests to be made public after use, the test publishers were there in force to protest. And when a weakened form of the bill finally passed, the companies moved to cut back their activities in New York. A lot of New York youngsters must bring their No. 2 pencils to New Jersey or Pennsylvania nowadays because of the companies' restricted testing schedule in New York. When a similar bill came before the Congress in 1979–1980, the companies were there too, led by the Educational Testing Service. A massive lobbying effort succeeded in having the bill set aside, though it may yet come up for reconsideration. Far from seeking a free and open evaluation of their product, the test publishers incur a lot of expense to avoid such public scrutiny.

The companies advance an explanation: To make the tests public would require using new tests every time, the cost of which would have to be borne by students. This argument is true as far as it goes, but it misses the point. No matter how much money can be saved, if a test is seriously defective, it should not be used at all for decisions about children's lives. And there is no way to evaluate a test properly as long as any professional who sees it must swear secrecy first.

The same situation as to secrecy prevails in competency testing. There too, the states put forward a cost argument to justify secrecy. But in minimum competency, the case is all the more compelling for making the tests public once they have been used. The decisions that depend on the test scores are extremely important, especially in those states where receipt of a diploma is conditional on passing the test. The doubtful quality of some minimum competency tests is even more reason to make them available for disinterested review.

The next chapter takes up the question of test quality in more detail. The issue is important, because the tests themselves are a limiting factor on how well the competency movement can carry out its mandate. If the tests are defective, then a great many students stand to be seriously wronged.

A Survey of the Problems with Competency Tests

Even with good tests, however, the movement's problems would be far from over. There remains the task of setting a cutoff score to mark the boundary between success and failure. That seems easy enough, at first glance — simply decide what skills are essential and place the cutoff accordingly. But there are complications of several kinds.

In most states, the test score merges the student's performance on a wide variety of tasks into one or two numbers. For example, a student might be able to pass a math section without knowing how to divide numbers if he does well enough on the other questions. The same score can represent many different skill combinations, so that it may not be possible for a single cutoff score to divide the student body into two meaningful and consistent groups.

In practice, though, such educational concerns play only a small part in setting minimum competency standards. As we shall see in Chapter 3, the political questions are usually far more important. The main political tension is simply stated: Educators are expected simultaneously to maintain high standards (high cutoff score) and to fail very few students (low cutoff score). These two requirements are inconsistent, at least in the short run. The task of choosing a cutoff score is often chiefly a matter of finding a politically acceptable compromise between the two priorities.

In the long run, the road out of the dilemma is to change curriculum, training more students to pass even when the standards are high. Such a move is exactly what most of the competency states intend. It would doubtless improve competency scores. But it would not improve education as a whole. Other goals of education are certain to suffer badly. For the large majority of students who are safely above the competency cutoff, score-raising efforts for the competency tests are likely to have severely adverse consequences. I shall take up these longer term effects in Chapter 4, using developments in math education as an example.

One of the important claims advanced for competency testing is its fairness to all students. Everyone takes the same test and is held to the same standards. And yet (without meaning to sound metaphysical), the same test is not the same test when different students take it. This is most obvious when a student is handicapped or speaks English as a second language. A test read aloud to a blind student, or even presented in Braille, is considerably more demanding than that which his sighted counterpart takes—even though the tests are otherwise identical. A test in English given to a Spanish-speaking child presents a different task than it does to an Anglo child.

Similarly, a white suburban child and a black youngster from the inner city do not take the same test. Competency tests are written in terms of the majority culture's usages and values. There are reasons in social policy for this practice, but they may not outweigh the disadvantage that it hands to minority students in the testing room. Chapter 5 explores these issues and other effects of minimum competency on minority and handicapped students.

Once a minimum competency program has been established by a state legislature or department, there are only two ways to get rid of it. The enacting body can change its mind, or the courts can declare some aspect of the test illegal. So far the legislatures and departments have not shown an inclination to reverse their decisions. But minimum competency testing is entering a period of great activity in the courts. Whether competency testing survives at all, and in what forms, will depend largely on court rulings over the next several years.

The legal issues involved are complex, especially in these early phases of litigation. Chapter 6 discusses some of the legal principles most likely to apply. Included in the chapter are cases bearing on two areas of the law with special pertinence to students who fail the tests: the school's legal duty to educate (there may not be any, as we shall see) and the question of unconstitutional discrimination by race.

With that background, Chapter 7 turns to a recent court decision that found certain aspects of the competency program in Florida to be unconstitutional. I shall take up that case in detail for two reasons. First, it is likely to influence the outcome of later suits; and second, the court looked carefully at many aspects of competency testing that deserve close attention on their own merits, quite apart from their legal implications.

Finally, Chapter 8 steps back to look at some of the longer-term effects that minimum competency testing may bring to society. They are not favorable, on the whole. There may indeed be fewer students in the future who cannot read and write. But if that improvement comes about, it will not be due to the tests themselves. Instead, it will result from changes that the schools make in order to satisfy the tests. We should try to anticipate what other effects these changes might bring.

The most serious outcome is likely to be an end to the quest for excellence in our schools. The testing scheme is meant to raise the floor of education—but it may bring down the ceiling as well.

Advocates insist that their programs specify only a minimum of competence and do not address the maximum at all. But the educational enterprise is more complicated than that. Its many parts, all tightly interwoven, tend to absorb any change by spreading it through the system. A competency test will make itself felt in classroom practice, textbook publication, teacher education and evaluation, audiovisuals, school supplies, and perhaps even the architecture of school buildings. All grade levels are certain to be affected, even in states that confine their testing to the high schools. In setting a minimum, legislation for competency testing triggers important changes in almost every aspect of elementary and secondary education. The program makes a simple enough demand—test the students—but the effects of that demand become quite complex, as we shall see.

Furthermore, when the school people read minimum competency legislation, they see something different from what the legislature thinks it wrote. The act, with all of its legislative and regulatory paraphernalia, addresses the issue of a minimum level of competence. All students should be barely able, at least, to read and write. To the schools, though, the instruction becomes slightly different: Turn out as many students as possible who can barely read and write. The legislature's "at least" is not really consistent with the goal of functional literacy for everyone. In practice, the schools can meet the legislation most efficiently by promoting mediocre work among a great many students. Excellent work by a smaller number—and only a few are capable of it—does not pay nearly so well, in a minimum competency environment.

These are not the times to speak of excellence. Even the word has an elitist fragrance. Excellence carries no weight politically. At a time when the national literacy is in doubt, when millions of high school graduates cannot read their own yearbooks, an educator who stands up for excellence is asking for trouble. Perhaps, as some say, the schools should not try to run until they can walk again.

Yet excellence is not something we can lightly set aside. We cannot afford to. Human problems are piling up faster than we can solve them. For the first time since men and women appeared on the earth, the survival of the race is in doubt—not just because of the threat of war, but now also because of man-made threats to atmosphere, ocean, and climate. It will help all of us, even the illiterates, if there are some very bright people in the next generation—people who like to think, like to work hard, and who don't mind confronting problems that look too big to handle.

These people are in school now. They need an education not just in reading and history and chemistry, but also in the satisfaction that comes from doing something worthwhile and doing it very well. They can learn this only from us, the adults. Adults decide what children will find important by encouraging them to achieve it. Despite television and peer pressure and all the rest, children still, for the most part, take their cues from parents and teachers.

We teach children how to do things well by insisting on excellence, by demanding the best that they can do. This is not news; parents and teachers have known this since the time of the prehistoric hunt. But in the rush to accept minimum competency testing, we seem to have forgotten it. In asking the least from the greatest number, we are not seeking nearly enough. It may produce a generation of children who can all play scales, but none of whom can play any music worth listening to.

Minimum competency testing erodes the quest for excellence in our schools. And this it must do in order to accomplish its goals—not deliberately, but by the inevitable side effects of what it seeks to accomplish. The test itself is nothing, but the test sets off a pattern of causes and effects that leaves no room for aspirations much higher than merely passing it. Regardless of the gains to literacy that competency testing might bring, we need, even more, to strive for the best. Not until the competency movement has run its course can we once again try for excellence in our schools.

Notes

1. In testing, there is a distinction between precision and accuracy. Test makers prefer the terms *reliability* and *validity,* respectively, and use them to make the same distinction. A test is reliable if it can discriminate consistently among students; it is valid if the discrimination it makes is the one the user expects. Chapter 2 discusses these terms in depth.

2. The error described here is that resulting from imperfect reliability and is reflected in the test's reliability coefficient. See Chapter 2 for details.

2
The Technology of Testing

W hatever else they may be, minimum competency tests are primarily a species of test. As such, they share the strengths and weaknesses of many other tests used in schools. They are unlikely to be much better than the bulk of the 1,500 or so achievement tests (Buros 1977) now on the market. Tests of "life skills" may be considerably worse.

Lately, established methods of testing in the schools have been subjected to a great deal of study (e.g., Houts 1977). Minimum competency tests, however, have not yet had the same kind of intense review, partly because they are relatively new and partly because of the security imposed by test publishers. There is no doubt that over the years to come, we shall see minimum competency tests subjected to much closer examination. But minimum competency tests represent no particular "breakthrough" in development that would markedly distinguish them from earlier tests. The newer ones are part of the same technological evolution that began early in the century with Binet's attempts to identify retarded children in the Parisian schools, matured during World War I with the Army Alpha Test for assigning recruits, and now provides a vast array of tests for school achievement, college and professional school admissions, and credential certification.

The development of minimum competency tests, despite their distinct purposes, for the most part relies on the same skills and procedures that have imperfectly served existing achievement tests for decades. Any problems that the industry has failed to solve in its long and active history are likely to remain unsolved in the present while the industry, and its less experienced colleagues in the state departments of education, takes on the relatively new task of devising tests to measure minimum competence.

Types of Tests

Tests differ in several respects, the most important differences being intended purpose, manner of reporting scores, and format (for example, essay, multiple choice, etc.). The test companies and their educator-clients maintain a clear terminology on these distinctions, but the popular press does not and so fosters considerable confusion. We shall see that the underlying reality may not be as clear as the professional terminology might imply. But as intelligent debate requires at least some agreement on what the words mean, a few definitions are essential.

Achievement Tests

Achievement tests try to measure what the child has learned in the past. Teacher-made tests are nearly always of achievement: What is ½ of ⅔? What were the causes of the Civil War? Circle all the words wrongly spelled. And so on. Likewise, tests that accompany a textbook series are designed to assess whether students have acquired the information or skills that the books try to convey.

Large-Scale Achievement Tests

Large-scale achievement tests attempt a similar goal on a regional or national basis. Examples are the Metropolitan Achievement Test, the Iowa Test of Basic Skills, and half a dozen other well-known "instruments"—a word that publishers prefer to "tests," perhaps because it connotes more precision.

Like teacher-made tests, large-scale achievement tests aim to find out what the child knows (presumably as a result of school instruction), but their content cannot be particular to a single classroom or text series. Rather, the questions (called "items" in the trade) come from the test publisher's best guess as to what most children are being taught. The publisher ordinarily reviews all the textbooks in common use and consults with several educators in the course of making these decisions. Nevertheless, such a test can give highly misleading results for a child whose instruction does not conform to the publisher's expectations. Averaged scores from these tests often appear in local newspapers and hence form an important input to public judgments about how well the schools are doing their job.

Aptitude Tests

Aptitude tests are intended for a different purpose entirely: to determine a student's capacity for future performance. Ideally, though impossible in practice, an aptitude test should not measure what the student has already learned but only his potential for further learning. Intelligence Quotient (IQ) tests, if they functioned properly, would fall squarely in this category. To a lesser extent, so might the Scholastic Aptitude Test (SAT), which most undergraduate colleges require of their applicants, the Law School Admissions Test (LSAT), and several others.

The SAT is called an aptitude test, not an achievement test, but here the distinction might not mean a great deal. Early in 1974, the public learned that average SAT scores had been declining nationally for the preceding ten years, in both the verbal and mathematical categories (College Entrance Examination Board 1977). This trend of steady decline in the SAT scores seems to be continuing, as shown by the results just out at this writing. In the furor that followed this unpleasant news came shrill complaints that the quality of public school education had declined. The College Entrance Examination Board (CEEB), which is ultimately responsible for the SAT, appointed a blue-ribbon panel to look into the matter. Chaired by former Secretary of Labor Willard Wirtz and including some of the best-known names in American education, the panel issued its report in 1977 (CEEB 1977) under the catchy title, "On Further Examination." The panel indeed found, amidst a multitude of other possible causes, that changes in schooling practice may have contributed to the decline in scores. Yet if the SAT were, as its title suggests, truly an aptitude test, students' scores should depend much more on their inherent aptitude than on their past education.

Of course, this makes no sense. A student's aptitude for college depends largely on success at earlier schooling, along with his or her interests, goals, motivation, study habits, maturity, and a host of other factors—none of which, incidentally, play any direct part in the SAT. At the very least, a student who missed learning to read and write with reasonable facility stands little chance of making it through freshman year. It is not possible, in short, to say meaningfully whether the SAT is an achievement test or an aptitude test. It can only be both.

In fact, it is safe to say that *all* educational tests measure some combination of achievement and aptitude, even if the test has one or the other of those words in its title (Levine 1976). Just as aptitude tests like the SAT must necessarily also measure achievement, achievement tests are likewise among the best indicators of aptitude for further learning. No test can fall wholly into one category or the other. The title of the test reflects not so much the nature of the test itself as the purposes for which it is most often used.

My former colleague at the Massachusetts Institute of Technology and Education Development Center in Newton, Massachusetts, Professor Judah L. Schwartz, once proposed a simple experiment: Print individual items from both achievement tests and aptitude tests on separate cards, then shuffle the cards and have people experienced in testing try to sort them back into the two categories (Schwartz 1977a, pp. 91–92). The task would almost certainly prove to be impossible, because items from the two kinds of tests are typically indistinguishable. This may well explain why aptitude tests can in fact give reasonably good predictions of achievement—when achievement is measured by tests that closely resemble the aptitude tests! (Zacharias 1977, p. 75).

Nonetheless, the supposed distinction between these two kinds of tests is important. The two are judged by different standards; that is, they are differently "validated," a matter I shall take up below. Test publishers often treat aptitude and achievement tests as if they were, in fact, fundamentally different.

Minimum Competency Tests

Minimum competency tests further confuse the distinction

between achievement and aptitude. In reality, they can be either one or both. In some jurisdictions the goal is to predict students' success at handling certain daily chores of adult life. This makes the test one of aptitude—though, like the SAT, it must also reflect past learning. But another common goal is to ascertain whether the student has learned skills taught in school, which is a function of achievement. Though people who develop the tests do not seem to have confronted the distinction directly, they do so implicitly in the course of validating particular tests for particular purposes. Indeed, much of the controversy on goals of minimum competency testing can be traced back to unspoken assumptions about aptitude versus achievement.

Norm-Referenced Tests

A second important way to distinguish tests is by whether they are norm referenced or criterion referenced. Norm-referenced tests compare individual students with a larger group, although the fact of comparison is not always obvious. A student's SAT score, for example, really indicates where the student stands among his peers and does not indicate his aptitude against any fixed standard.[1] The SAT is one example of a norm-referenced test. It is not quite correct to say, as some authors do, that such tests compare students with one another. The comparison is always with a large group to which the student may or may not belong. Typically, the comparison is with a "standardization group" that took the test some years earlier.

IQ tests are a second example of norm referencing. Indeed, the average IQ for any age group is arbitrarily fixed at 100. Other IQ numbers are assigned symmetrically on either side of 100, using a mathematical formula that puts about half the age group between IQs of 90 and 110, and about 90 percent between 75 and 125. In the end, whatever an IQ test says about someone's intelligence (which might be very little), it says it only in comparison with other people of the same age group.

Until the past few years, school achievement tests were nearly always norm referenced. So-called standardized tests, in particular, are just norm-referenced tests scored in comparison with a carefully picked sample of students.

Any test that reports in "percentiles," as most achievement

tests used to, is norm referenced. A percentile is the percentage of students in the same grade who did the same or worse than the student in question; it is *not* the percentage of items answered correctly. For example, a student in the 60th percentile did better than 59 percent of his grade-mates, worse than 40 percent, and about the same as 1 percent.

Many critics have pointed out that percentile scores and other norm-referenced scores are of limited value: They tell nothing of the child's individual achievement, except in comparison with the group. Unless little Sammy's or Susie's parents have a pretty good idea of how well third graders read nationwide, the fact that third-grader Sammy or Susie was in the 73rd percentile is not very helpful, except perhaps for boasting to the neighbors.

Grade-equivalent scores, an especially pernicious form of norm referencing, figure extensively in discussions of minimum competency testing. The explanation of these scores is a little complicated. Let us imagine giving a fourth-grade mathematics test to students in grades ranging from first to tenth. We figure a separate average score for each grade. Then we give the same test to a fourth grader. But instead of reporting his own score, we report the grade in which the average score was the same as his. Thus, if Sammy in the fourth grade got 68 items right, and 68 was also the average score in the fifth grade, his teacher might say, "Sammy is doing math at the fifth-grade level." That would be wrong, though; Sammy is doing fourth-grade math as well as a fifth-grader, which is a very different thing from fifth-grade math (Weber 1974).

The whole business, in fact, is fundamentally ambiguous. Take a twelfth grader who is said to be reading at the ninth-grade level. Does this mean he or she is (1) getting a ninth-grade score on a twelfth-grade test, or (2) getting an average score on a ninth-grade test? And if it is the latter, does that average score come from just ninth-grade students, or from students in other grades as well? In the manner that most grade-equivalent scores are reported, there is no way to answer these questions. Yet the answers would make a great difference.

In Florida, for example, in early trials of the competency exam, some of the best high school juniors tested at a distressingly low grade level. One explanation turned out to be simple: The test was designed for lower grades and included material these students had not worked with for several years, such as computing with decimals. Some students had simply forgotten how (Haney and Madaus 1978*a*). Presumably this group would have done much better on a tenth-grade test. In this case, the grade-equivalent score might vary by several years depending on the test given — with a better score on a supposedly more difficult test!

There is another complication. When scores are reported in grade equivalents, possible test errors become extremely large for children who do much better or much worse than the average. A child who scores several grades higher or lower than his school grade can shift his test score by another full grade or more by answering only one or two items differently. For children in the middle of the range, on the other hand, one or two additional correct items will have very little effect. This "sensitivity at the extremes" calls for extra care in interpreting scores of children doing exceptionally poorly or exceptionally well, as minor chance factors can alter their scores dramatically. Percentile test scores are less subject to this problem because they magnify this kind of test error less than grade equivalents do. But it would be a serious mistake to use, say, a twelfth-grade test for minimum competence with the cutoff placed several grade equivalents lower; there would be serious risk of error. Using a lower level test, on the other hand, exposes students to the possibility of having forgotten earlier material, as in the Florida case.

Ordinarily we do not think of minimum competency tests as reporting in grade equivalents. Much of the discussion surrounding them, however, uses that terminology. For example, minimum competency advocates sometimes say that a high school graduate should be able to read "at an eighth-grade level." Does this mean as well as the average eighth-grader, or as well as a high school graduate who scores a grade equivalent of eight? As the appropriate test in each case is different, answers to this question will have a bearing on who graduates.

It is also important to note that nearly half of all students nationwide are performing below grade level — not through any fault of their education, but simply because of how grade equivalents are defined. This widespread "failure" is a consequence of the mathematics of scoring and would remain the case no matter how good the schools are. Less informed participants in the testing controversy occasionally demand that standards be set at the twelfth-grade level. "We're paying for twelve years of education," said one, "and we're only getting eight." If implemented, this suggestion would simply deny diplomas to just under half of all high school seniors. The misunderstanding results from ignorance of how the scoring system works but also points up the fundamentally misleading nature of grade-equivalent scores.

Criterion-Referenced Tests

Criterion-referenced tests try to avoid the problems inherent in percentiles and grade equivalents. Instead of comparing children to their grade-mates, criterion referencing compares each student's achievement to some fixed standard, or criterion. A student simply passes or fails each section of the test according to how many items he or she answers correctly. The score does not depend on how well other students do, as in norm-referenced tests.

In practice it is not hard to convert a test from one scoring method to the other, although the results of doing so are seldom satisfactory. A test publisher can take a norm-referenced achievement test from the shelf, establish a cutoff score for each section, and retitle it criterion referenced. Some publishers are reputed to have done just that in the early 1970s, when criterion referencing first came into style. On the other hand, a publisher could give a criterion-referenced test to many students, compile the results, and report scores thereafter in percentiles or grade equivalents.

It is far better, however, to design a test from the outset for either norm or criterion referencing, and that is now the usual practice. The outcomes of the two types of test are rather different. Primarily aiming to discriminate among students, a norm-referenced test will include few items that are extremely easy or extremely hard. It may also have several items that do not seem to test anything important, but which, according to the data, help to sort children into percentiles efficiently. A criterion-referenced test, on the other hand, will focus mostly on content that the test authors think is important for children to know and will sometimes explore that content in useful detail. The very best criterion-referenced tests not only give an indication of the child's performance, but also try to suggest where the child may be having particular trouble. In the current jargon, these tests are "diagnostic."

Criterion-referenced tests are more informative than norm-referenced, on the whole, but do not necessarily satisfy educators' needs. Later in this chapter I shall explore some of the defects common to many achievement tests. Most of these defects, we shall see, apply to criterion-referenced tests along with norm-referenced tests and are likely to affect minimum competency tests as well.

Advocates of minimum competency tests unanimously describe the tests as criterion referenced. According to the prevailing view, the tests seek to determine whether or not a student has acquired a particular body of skills, without regard to how many of his or her classmates have done so.

Matters are not that simple, in practice. To pick a standard and enforce it, with no regard to how many students can achieve that standard, would not work politically. If nearly all students can meet the standard, there is no need to have it at all. And if too many cannot, citizens will have every right to claim that the schools are failing to serve their children. An expert has summarized the problem this way:

> How many students can your school or state afford to remediate—or not promote or not graduate if remediation fails—afford both economically and politically? About 10%, more or less? Certainly it isn't 20%, the percent failing competency tests in many places today. Say it is 5%. Whatever it is, the percent failing the test will probably be higher. If you can't raise students to meet the minimum, will you lower the minimum to meet the students? Those are the only two ways to guarantee that 95% will succeed (Bricknell 1978, p. 32).

Dr. Bricknell speaks an unpleasant truth. It means, in the end, that minimum competency tests must be norm referenced after all, to the extent that standards must reflect allowable percentages of students failing. A cynic might say we should first decide how many students to fail and then pick standards so as to fail them. Political requirements dictate almost exactly that procedure. As a practical matter, there is no other course available. (The question of standards comes up for detailed examination in the following chapter.)

Measures of Test Quality

Tests can be good, bad, or indifferent. Like other manufactured products, they have their own standards of performance. Three of the important measures in assessing tests are *objectivity, reliability,* and *validity.*

At the outset, I should stress that these words take on different meanings in the context of testing than they do in ordinary English. An objective test need not treat students alike; a reliable test cannot necessarily be relied upon; and a valid test may not give meaningful results. Indeed, a test can be objective, reliable, and valid — as test makers use these words — and still be a very poor test.

Objective tests are those that students take under similar conditions and that are graded or "scored" uniformly. The first condition is relatively easy to meet in practice by making sure that all students have the same materials available, the same test instructions, the same amount of time, and so forth. Environmental factors like ventilation, lighting, noise level — even composition of the working surface — can also influence results (Lyman 1978, p. 37).

The condition of uniform grading is more difficult to meet. Essay tests are seldom objective, for example, because it is likely that any two graders will judge the same essay differently, and that both will shift their criteria as they work down through the pile of papers. Even short-answer tests can be hard to grade objectively. An oddball answer might be very wrong, or very right with a creative twist — and judges can well disagree on which it is.

Partly to overcome these problems, and partly because it allows cheap scoring by machine, the multiple-choice format has come to dominate educational testing. Objective tests and multiple-choice tests are practically synonymous to many educators. With only rare exceptions, the minimum competency movement seems also to have settled on multiple choice and similar formats (Haney and Madaus 1979*b*, p. 26).

Even a fully objective test is "fair" only in the sense that it is equally unfair to everyone taking it. A test may be ambiguous, wrongheaded, open to argument, even downright erroneous in the answers it counts as correct but can be an objective test nonetheless. For example,

How tall was Macbeth?

(a) 4 gallons

(b) 3 pounds

(c) 6 acres

(d) 2 hours

(Lazarus 1977*a*, p. 185)

The question itself is nonsensical; the available answers are hopelessly wrong for the question — and yet this item is perfectly objective.

Objectivity itself is a minor virtue, important chiefly in its contribution to reliability and validity. Objectivity comes at a cost, however. Because some kinds of knowledge and skill are much easier to test objectively than others, these tend to dominate the tests. An objective test of "citizenship," for example, might easily degenerate to relatively trivial questions on branches of government because broader and deeper issues of citizenship do not translate well into multiple-choice questions. Much the same is true in other subject areas. Even an objective test item in consumer math, such as finding the best buy in canned pineapple, is a very different task from dodging toddlers in the supermarket while keeping track of which cans in each brand are sliced, chunked, or crushed. Multiple-choice tests, in short, are a poor substitute for life. They are cheap to score, though.

The *reliability* of a test is a measure of certain kinds of test error. Suppose we could give a student the same test twice, without his or her learning anything the first time that would affect the score the second time. (In practice we cannot, but there are ways to approximate the experiment.) Chances are the student's scores on the two occasions would be different, even though his or her knowledge and skills are presumably the same. Motivation and alertness can vary. Time of day may be a factor. The student might guess differently on items he is unsure of, make different errors in reading or in arithmetic, or recall facts differently. As the score can vary even when the student's real "achievement" is fixed, the score cannot be a perfect measure of the achievement. The test, in other words, is subject to error.

Susceptibility to this kind of chance variation is expressed in a test's *reliability coefficient.* Higher coefficients are better, with a coefficient of 1.00 representing a perfect test. At the other extreme, if a test's coefficient were zero, its score would bear no relation whatsoever to the child's achievement. Well-established achievement tests usually show coefficients slightly above .90, with about .93 or .94 as the practical maximum. Many sorts of error are possible, however, which do not show up in the reliability coefficient, so that even a high coefficient does not necessarily bespeak a good test. A reliable test is a consistent one, but it still may not give meaningful results.

Publishers nowadays seldom measure reliability by the test/retest method sketched above. Instead they typically give students two forms of the same test, relying on the forms to be equivalent. Or else they split one test in two, sometimes just by adding up separate scores from the even-numbered and odd-numbered items, and compare the two scores. In either case — and there are other methods also — the reliability coefficient is computed from pairs of scores from many students. As in any experiment, there is always a margin of error in the reliability coefficient itself — error in the error, so to speak. To obtain a reasonably precise estimate of the reliability coefficient, and hence of possible error in the test, the reliability studies must include substantial numbers of students, and the students must faithfully represent those who will eventually be using the test.

Test makers routinely eliminate items that tend to lower reliability, that is, items on which a student is likely to give inconsistent answers on different occasions. There is an argument for doing so, as such items contribute less useful information to the final score than those that give more consistent results. Also dropped are items that show no improvement from grade to grade. Items answered incorrectly by students scoring high on the test as a whole, or those answered correctly by students scoring poorly, are likewise edited out (Jencks 1978). But all of this item-weeding may filter out important content as well. Just as some ideas are difficult to handle in multiple-choice format under any circumstances, others are hard to examine with mathematically consistent results.

It is a key policy issue whether to leave out such ideas from minimum competency testing altogether. To what extent should format control content? The issue brings to mind the ancient philosophical debates on form versus substance. Most states with minimum competency programs have implicitly chosen a side, though I have not seen the issue discussed in this particular form. To date, the consensus seems to be that format, and the economics that come with it, will largely dictate content. One result is likely to be a shift of concern away from the content and toward the limited techniques available to measure it (Haney and Madaus 1979*b*, p. 26).

Objectivity and reliability are both properties of a test taken in isolation. Neither measure speaks to how well a test can meet its intended purpose when administered to the people for whom it was designed. That is why a test can be both objective and reliable, yet still be a poor test. Even a test that is excellent for some purposes will necessarily be unsuitable for others, so the evaluation of a test must ultimately take into account what its users expect the test to accomplish.

Validity, the most important single property of a test, indicates how well the test actually measures what it claims to measure. Reliability and objectivity are of interest mainly because they can contribute to validity. Unfortunately, validity is also the most difficult property to assess with any degree of confidence. It is simple enough to tell whether a test is objective or not, and its reliability coefficient can always be determined through experiment. But in considering validity, subjective factors often play a decisive role.

Validity, in short, is a slippery subject requiring a great deal of caution. Test publishers use an impressive-sounding vocabulary that sometimes conveys the implication that validity stands on a much surer footing than it actually does. Here I shall briefly explore that vocabulary and the corresponding techniques for establishing validity. Each technique, by custom, is named as if it addressed a distinct kind of validity but all try to answer the same underlying question: Does the test do what it claims to?

Face validity is the simplest method for determining whether a test is valid. A test is "face valid"—literally, valid on its face—if it simply looks like a good test. Sometimes this makes sense. If a piece of paper looks like a test of addition or subtraction, then it probably is. But face validity is less clear for multiple-choice tests of "writing skills," for example, and even less so for more complex human topics like the social sciences and citizenship.

Content validity, a more sophisticated variant of face validity, presupposes that an expert has analyzed the content of the test and found it appropriate. A test of writing skills, for example, would be declared content valid if an expert on the teaching of writing determined that skills required for mastery of the test correspond to the skills required in writing. Note that this is still validation by opinion, albeit by expert opinion. But sometimes the expert who certifies the test is the same person whom the publisher paid to write it. Content validity can thus become a formality, so a publisher's announcement of content validity is not an unimpeachable indication of test quality.

The notion of content validity presumes a certain uniformity of curriculum wherever the test is used. Suppose, for example, that one school district teaches history from a social point of view, examining historical events in light of contemporary social developments, and another takes a predominantly cause-and-effect political approach. It is difficult to see how the same test could be content valid for both.

Predictive validity would be a far better method of judging tests, if it worked well. Take another imaginary experiment: Suppose we give a high-school-leaving test on "life skills" to a large sample of seniors and later, somehow, quantify their degrees of "survival" in the world as adults. We could then look back to see how well their test scores predicted survival. A test that made the prediction accurately would have a high degree of predictive validity.

That experiment remains to be performed. Researchers in the testing field, however, have carried out similar experiments based on other kinds of tests. With most of the tests used, it seems reasonable to expect a decent degree of prediction: a test of clerical skills predicting completion of a secretarial course, LSAT predicting first-year grades in law school, and so on. Certainly, studies of validity using these tests would seem more promising than studies using a minimum competency test to predict adult success, or even adult survival. Yet their results are discouraging.

The findings of such experiments are summarized in a *validity coefficient,* which expresses how effectively the test predicted for a large number of students. As with the reliability coefficient, a finding of 1.00 would be perfect, but Lee Cronbach (1970, p. 135), a widely respected expert in the field, says, "It is unusual for a validity coefficient to rise above 0.60, though that is far from perfect prediction." One series of LSAT experiments, for example, yielded coefficients between 0.25 and 0.40; these rose to a maximum range of 0.38 to 0.55 when the prediction took into account college grades as well as the LSAT. Results were only 0.47 in the secretarial experiment (Cronbach 1970, pp. 136–138).

Such coefficients are indeed far from perfect prediction. Figure 2.1 shows results from an imaginary experiment whose validity coefficient was 0.50, which would be unusually high for an actual experiment. These data actually came from a computer but look very similar to those that would appear in a successful experiment on predictive validity. In Figure 2.1, each little dot stands for one student. Each student's dot is placed along the bottom axis according to the student's test score and along the side axis according to the student's later success.

If the test predicted perfectly, all of the dots would fall

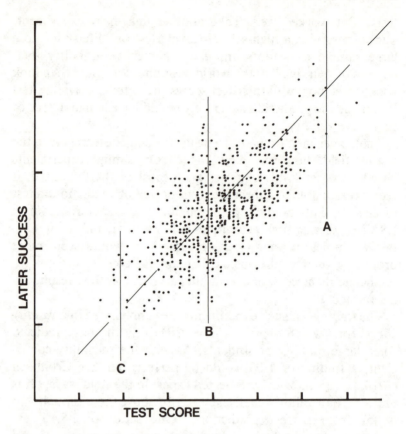

Figure 2.1. Relationship between test scores and later success, when the validity coefficient is 0.50.

Source: Adapted with permission from Zacharias 1977.

precisely along the dashed line. That would give a validity coefficient of 1.00; knowing individual students' test scores, we could then predict their success with absolute certainty. Because the dots scatter away from the dashed line, however, the prediction is less certain. The more they scatter, the worse the prediction and the lower the validity coefficient. If the coefficient were zero, the dots would make a formless cloud. In this diagram, the validity coefficient is 0.50, which corresponds to a particular degree of scatter.

Using the diagram, we can try to make predictions from three test scores. For a very high score, corresponding to the vertical line at A, the prediction is reasonably certain; the few people who scored near the A-line all come near the top of the diagram, which means they had considerable success after the test. Likewise, students who did poorly on the test, falling near the C-line, also did poorly afterward, as shown by their low placement on the diagram.

Consider a middling student, however, whose test score corresponds to the line at B. Notice two things. First, he has plenty of company. Most students score somewhere around the middle on most tests, because the tests are designed to produce that result. Second, students who scored near the B-line show a considerable diversity of success afterward. Despite their similar test scores, some did quite well and some quite poorly.

For the majority of students who fall near the middle, then, it appears that a validity coefficient of 0.50 is insufficient to make the test very useful as a predictive device.[2] And most of the tests that have been studied this way show lower coefficients, which means more scatter. Predictive validity, although usually considered "better" than face validity or content validity in evaluating tests, hardly gives satisfactory results.

Concurrent validity is a close relative of predictive validity. Instead of comparing test scores with events that occur later on, this procedure compares scores with other results obtained at approximately the same time as the test. Such an experiment might, for example, compare scores from a minimum competency test with job ratings of students who were employed. (There would be serious problems in designing the experiment. For example, employed students are a special group to begin with, and their different employers are unlikely to rate them uniformly.) Studies of concurrent validity also yield validity coefficients, which fall in roughly the same range as those of predictive validity.

Another form of concurrent validity compares results from the test in question to other measures of the same skill. If the other measure is also a test of some sort, then its validity must be examined as well. For some skills, however, it is possible to compare test results with the student's actual performance of the skill being tested. One example is writing. Are the students who write well, according to the usual school standards, the same students who do well on multiple-choice tests of writing skills? The answer, unfortunately, is that often they are not; the correlation between test scores and actual writing ability is very low (Haney and Madaus 1979*b*, p. 26).

In discussing typical results from predictive and concurrent validation, Cronbach (1970, p. 135) offers a frequently heard defense: "Although we would like higher coefficients, any positive correlation indicates that predictions from the test will be more accurate than guesses." Cronbach is undoubtedly right. There is a problem, nonetheless, if test users fail to recognize the limitations inherent in low coefficients. Because test scores have a scientific, no-nonsense look about them, users may tend to regard the scores as much more accurate than guesses, when sometimes they are only a little more accurate. Moreover, the mathematics raises the coefficients disproportionately if the prediction is accurate for relatively few students at the extremes—just where test error tends to be highest, and where the majority of students are not represented.

I shall mention *construct validity* only to say that it presently has no meaningful bearing on minimum competency tests. Some psychological theories employ "constructs," that is, properties assumed to influence behavior even though they cannot be observed directly. Two examples are intelligence and anxiety; we can see what we call intelligent behavior and anxious behavior, but not the underlying constructs of intelligence and anxiety themselves. A test whose scores match up reasonably well with other tests for such constructs is said to have *construct validity*. Perhaps someone will eventually develop a theoretical construct called "adult competence" or the like and validate a test against it. Until then, and maybe even after, we can safely overlook this form of validation.

Curricular validity requires that the content of a test actually be part of the students' curriculum. If a test has curricular validity, it examines what students in a particular school, district, or state are expected to learn. Questions about curricular validity first arose with the growth of nationally distributed achievement tests. Because thousands of local school districts, each with its own curriculum, drew from the same handful of tests, there was sometimes question as to whether particular tests matched up with particular courses of study. If they did not, of course, the test would be patently unfair to the students involved.

One good example of problems with curricular validity appeared in elementary mathematics during the early 1970s. At that time, some school districts were still committed to "new math," others were phasing it out in favor of "back to basics," and a few latecomers were still phasing it in. The publishers tried to balance content in their tests according to some sort of national average of curriculum, but chances are that few students were tested according to the content they actually encountered in school. Some districts, on the other hand, solved the problem by continually adjusting their curricula to keep pace with the changing tests.

The question of curricular validity is very pertinent to minimum competency testing. Some companies are distributing minimum competency tests on a national scale, and many statewide tests are in use. Yet local districts still maintain the prerogative of setting curriculum, which raises the possibility that tests will not match curricula.

Merle McClung, an attorney interested in minimum competency testing, claims that a school system that denied diplomas without establishing curricular validity would be on shaky legal ground if challenged by a disgruntled student (McClung 1977). He argues further that curricular validity is not enough. Schools may also have to show what McClung calls *instructional validity:* that students are actually exposed to sufficient classroom instruction in the knowledge and skills being tested. Otherwise, he says, the test is "arguably so arbitrary as to violate due process of law" (McClung 1978). I shall take up these legal issues more thoroughly in a later chapter.

These several forms of validation fall in three categories: *validation by opinion* (face and content); *validation by comparison* (predictive, concurrent, and construct); and *validation by practice* (curricular and instructional). It should be clear, however, that no one of these can assure that a test is doing its job. And even if a test could be validated by several of these methods, which is rarely possible, it would still be no guarantee of meaningful results. A test can be silly, trivial, and even largely wrong, yet still carry impressive certifications of validity.

Furthermore, a test properly validated for a group can still give invalid results for particular students. It is elementary statistics that group results can show one thing and individual results something else entirely. Yet the sanctions that follow from minimum competency testing apply to individuals, though justification for the test nearly always comes from group data (Airasian 1979, p. 36). Suppose we could prove a minimum competency test valid for 99 students out of 100. Is it justifiable afterward to claim that the test is valid for most other people, while we apply sanctions against the 100th student? The question can take on real meaning in the cases of minority group and handicapped students, another topic I must defer to a different chapter.

Such questions remain secondary, however. The present art of testing raises doubts about validity not just for a few students but for nearly all. Whatever confidence may come from reading publishers' materials on validity often evaporates with a study of the test items themselves. Some educators, it seems, are willing to approve foolish-looking test items on the basis of publishers' statistical data, and test security often makes the items unavailable for inspection, leaving only the data to review. Yet no amount of computer printout can turn a bad item into a good one.

Other Defects in Tests

A few years ago, before the rise of minimum competency testing, two colleagues and I reviewed most of the standardized achievement tests then in widespread use.[3] These particular tests represented the pinnacle of the test makers' skill at the time. All the tests had been thoroughly reviewed by panels of experts, most had passed through several editions over decades of experience, and all had undergone evaluation with thousands of students. Yet in a few days of reading, we found dozens of apparently defective items. The overall nature and format of the tests also raised troubling questions.

It may be that minimum competency tests will escape such problems, but it seems unlikely. Clearing all of the bugs from a test takes time and experience, and most minimum competency tests have been in use for only a few years or less. If the test publishers, with all of their available expertise and resources, cannot manage a reasonably clean instrument, it will be surprising if a state testing office with its limited resources can do a great deal better. The "state of the art" is just not sufficiently advanced.

The following is a brief catalog of the most common defects in current tests. All of the defects listed apply, to a varying extent, to all of the competency tests I have examined.

Inappropriate content. Any test can sample only particular content within a subject area. The test results depend solely on that sample, which is often severely limited by the format of the test. Despite allegations of content validity and curricular validity, tests often do not fairly represent the larger body of content they are supposed to examine.

Need for reading and linguistic skills. Before a written test is a test of consumer math or career awareness or anything else, it is first of all a reading test, usually in a compact and stylized form of English. Even if testers are willing to let lack of reading skills pull down scores in other areas, which seems unfair, it would be even more unjust to demand better reading skills in tests of other subjects than in tests of reading.

Frequent incorrectness. Many existing tests, including some of the most respected, have serious mistakes in subject matter, both wrong answers counted right and perfectly reasonable answers counted wrong. This puts a special burden on students who know the subject matter extremely well because they must put their knowledge aside and attempt to figure out what the test author wants.

Ambiguity and lack of clarity. Many tests have items that are unnecessarily obscure or frankly ambiguous. For example,

Mark P for an error in punctuation, C for an error in capitalization, G for an error in grammar, and N for no error. [excerpt from instructions for this question]

A. Have you ever went to a flea

B. market. Sandmore High School will have the

C. second International Flea Market on Saturday.

(Sample question from "Proficiency and Review" test in Denver, Colorado, quoted in Southeastern Public Education Program 1978, p. 12)

I am honestly at a loss as to whether *second* in line C should be capitalized. Is the word part of a title, or simply an adjective?

Clerical emphasis. Most competency tests, especially at the upper grade levels, require students to shade in little squares or ovals on separate answer sheets. This makes machine scoring less expensive. But students who are sloppy or careless on their answer sheets will receive low scores even if they know the answers to most of the questions.

Time pressure. Many tests are timed, putting students who freeze under stress at a marked disadvantage. Yet, supposedly, calmness under pressure is not a trait being tested.

Inflexibility. Different people think in different ways, but multiple-choice tests make no allowance for individuality. A creative answer is almost always wrong, and a sense of humor only leads to trouble.

No credit for partial understanding. Multiple-choice answers are either right or wrong; answers are never more correct or less correct. Even when a student can eliminate all the wrong answers but two, if he guesses incorrectly he will still receive the same score of zero as another student who has no idea what the question is about.

Lack of diagnosis. One often-stated purpose of minimum competency testing is to identify students who need help. Simply identifying students is of little value, however, without some guidance as to what kind of help is needed. Very few tests on the market are diagnostically useful, and the need for diagnosis seems to have been overlooked altogether in most of the current minimum competency programs.

Cultural and linguistic bias. Any written document, including a test, must take certain linguistic usages for granted. That in turn implies some degree of commonality in background and experience. Many students, however, including minority group students as well as others, may bring different meanings to the words and phrases than test authors assume they will. Such students thus have the extra task of decoding the questions to figure out what they might mean in someone else's language and culture.

Of these defects, some can be cured through more careful test authorship and review. Others, however, are inherent in the multiple-choice format and allow less room for improvement.

Taking into account not only the defects in individual items, but also the uncertainties in reliability and validation, the picture on the whole is discouraging. Even if the technology of testing were sufficiently advanced as to make excellent instruments available, there would still be questions about the wisdom of using the tests as the sole basis for decisions so important as promotion from grade to grade and the awarding of high school diplomas. With doubts about whether the test results are meaningful, the situation is far worse. The risks of using such tests as the major basis for school reform are great.

A workman, the saying goes, is no better than his tools. The minimum competency movement cannot be better than its tests. It cannot do well by its students with the testing art as it presently stands, and unfortunately, there is no reason to think that our ability to test students will suddenly improve within the next several years.

Notes

1. More precisely, a student taking the SAT is compared with students who took the test in 1941 (Lyman 1978, p. 95). Before 1941, students taking the test each year were "normed" only against each other. If that practice had continued, there would be no way to tell, without re-analysis, whether performance on the test improved or declined over the years. The continual renorming would have kept the average score at 500 year after year, even if average performance were changing over that time.

2. I am indebted for this discussion to Jerrold Zacharias, who pointed out to me these properties of imperfect correlations during a session in his office one afternoon. Zacharias has since published the explanation in a paper on IQ testing (1977), which I have followed closely in preparing this chapter.

3. Our proposal resulted in the first of several grants to Education Development Center for what is now Project TORQUE. Written in collaboration with Judah L. Schwartz and Jerrold R. Zacharias, with valuable assistance from Edwin F. Taylor, the proposal spun off several papers generally critical of standardized achievement testing (Lazarus 1977*a*; Schwartz 1977*b*; Taylor 1977*b*; and Taylor and Schwartz 1977). Paul Houts, editor of *Principal,* published these papers together with others in a special issue of the magazine entitled "The Scoring of Children" and later collected them in a book (Houts 1977). When response to the magazine issue indicated a widely felt need for further study on the questions raised, Zacharias and Houts, along with Vito Perrone of the North Dakota Study Group on Evaluation, founded the National Consortium on Testing. The consortium has since emerged as a major national forum, with a membership at this writing of 49 organizations active in education and testing.

3

Setting Standards
for Minimum Competency

S *cene: Corridor in a public building. Enter Politician and*
Educator.

Politician: I don't understand what you're so worried about.
You've got three years before the law takes effect. Can't you
have the tests ready by then?

Educator: Sure we could, if we knew what to test for. But it
may take us a while to figure that out.

Politician: The law looks clear enough to me. You just have to
test the kids every few grades and make sure they have the
skills they need. Pardon my saying so, but that's something
you should have been doing all along.

Educator: We *have* been doing it all along, districtwide on a reg-
ular schedule. But the problems are a lot more complicated
than you make them sound. That's the trouble here—you're
trying to solve a problem you don't understand simply by
passing a law. Now we educators still have to solve the problem, and we have to make your law work at the same time.

Politician: Don't blame us for the law—the voters demanded it.
If you people had done your job right in the first place and
kept the test scores up, this never would have happened.
We're just trying to help you get things straightened out, back
the way they used to be.

Educator: Actually, the test scores *have* stayed up, at least in the really basic skills—the same ones you want us to test for.[1] What has declined are the more complex skills. But your new law doesn't even mention those.

Politician: Maybe I shouldn't say this, but from a political standpoint it doesn't matter if the test scores have gone up or down or sideways. All that matters is that the public thinks the kids aren't learning enough. Besides, if what you say is true, the kids should do fine on the new tests. Just make sure they all pass, and there's nothing to worry about.

Educator: Make *all* the kids pass? I don't think you understand. Sure, we can write a test everybody will pass, but you won't like it.

Politician: We'll go along with anything reasonable. After all, you're the experts in this business, not us. All we want is some assurance that a high school graduate can balance his check book and read what he has to, that sort of thing.

Educator: I wish it were that easy. Tell me, what should everybody be able to read? Not this law of yours, I hope.

Politician: Oh, come on, be reasonable. The kids should be able to read the things they're going to run across in daily life. You know, the newspaper, that sort of thing.

Educator: All right, let's start with the newspaper. The *Wall Street Journal* or the *National Enquirer?* The editorials or the comics?

Politician: I don't care much. As long as they can read, I don't see that it matters *what* they read.

Educator: It makes a big difference. We have to test everybody at some specific reading level. It's fine to say, "As long as they can read," but someone has to decide exactly what that means.

Politician: Aim high, then. Isn't that the way to get results? If everybody could read the *Wall Street Journal,* maybe I'd get less crackpot mail on the economic issues.

Educator: You'd get a lot more mail on education, though. Do you know what will happen if we set the standards that high?

Politician: I think so. We'll hear some complaints from you educationists, or whatever you call yourselves nowadays. But once you realize that everybody else in the state wants good results, and you hold a wet finger to the wind on your bond issues, I expect you'll find a way to do it.

Educator: Do you realize you're asking for something close to a twelfth-grade reading level?

Politician: Sure, why not? If a kid goes to school through the twelfth grade, he ought to be able to read at the twelfth-grade level when he graduates. If he can't, you're really letting the taxpayers down.

Educator: But twelfth-grade reading level is just an average. That means the middle. Half the kids are below the middle; that's why it's the middle. Are you following me? If we put the standard there, then half the kids will fail. That means a lot of angry kids and parents. Voters, too.

Politician: I see what you mean. All right, forget the *Wall Street Journal*. Suppose we just say all the kids should be able to read—well, what would you pick?

Educator: Whatever we pick, some kids won't be able to do it. We have some kids in high school who can barely get through a third-grade book.

Politician: I know. That's why we passed this law.

Educator: But there are kids we can't help much, no matter what we do. Some just don't have the smarts, though we use fancy names for that. Some have real trouble at home, problems you and I can't do anything about. Quite a few don't get enough to eat, or they drink heavily or take drugs. And some have parents who think school is a government plot—you wouldn't believe some of the stories we hear.

Politician: Those are exceptions, aren't they? Aren't most kids perfectly capable of doing their schoolwork, if they just try hard enough? You haven't been giving them the incentive, that's the problem.

Educator: It's the people you call exceptions who are going to be hardest hit by this law. We had one kid last year with a bad drug problem and no way to pay for it but to prostitute himself on the street. Then his mother comes in, a very sweet woman, and she wants to know why he's failing algebra. We have little girls thirteen years old getting pregnant, kids getting knifed after school, everything you can imagine. These people are in no shape to sit at home and diagram sentences. What happens to them?

Politician: Look, there are places kids can go if they need help. We have one of the best juvenile programs in the country. I don't mean to sound callous, but that's not the problem we're concerned with right now.

Educator: It is, though. These are just the people who'll never get a high school diploma, according to your new law. In fact, they'll drop out in droves. If you think you have a welfare problem now, wait till you've declared a whole class of citizens officially unfit for employment.

Politician: All right, you have a point. But if somebody can't even read the want ads, he can't find a job anyway. Say, would that satisfy you as a standard?

Educator: It's a lot more realistic, as long as you understand that we're still going to lose some kids. We don't use want ads much in school, though. We've always preferred books, but I suppose we can switch over. All that vacant library space will come in handy.

Politician: That's ridiculous. Reading is reading. Nobody says you should stop using books. If they can read books, they can read want ads. What you're saying completely misinterprets the law.

Educator: I know it does, but you're forcing us to that. We have a lot of students who can read books but will have trouble with want ads. Give me your paper. Look here, "Sales mgr rtl exp pt tm eves near trans 8K + comm." We can teach that if you want us to, and we'll get most of the kids to pass the test on it. It's not real reading, but if it's what the public is going to judge us by, that's where we have to put the effort. It's a matter of limited resources.

Politician: Just a minute, now. Your job is to teach basic reading. Want ads are part of that. That's exactly what this law is about, redirecting your effort toward the basics.

Educator: That redirection, as you call it, is planning for failure, not success. Most students already master the basics. A lot of them get into Shakespeare, good novels, all kinds of things. Under the law, though, we'll be hurting ourselves if we keep that up. Instead, you're telling us to put everything we have on the few kids who might otherwise fail the test.

Politician: Nobody says you should do that. It would make a travesty of education.

Educator: Then you should have put real money into the law, not just funds for the testing. Without cutting back somewhere, we can't add on the new instruction we'll need for want ads and whatever else goes in the reading test, not to mention the writing, math, consumer education, and all the rest. And we haven't even mentioned remediation for the kids who fail. Do you have any idea what that's going to cost?

Politician: You know why we can't put in more money right now. That's why we need this law in the first place—the public thinks they're not getting their money's worth as it is. But you should look at this as an opportunity, a chance to rebuild public confidence in the schools. For the first time, you'll be able to prove your success. Once people are convinced that the schools are doing the job, then we can reexamine all the issues you raise.

Educator: And in the meantime?

Politician: In the meantime, the best thing you can do is design tests that look appropriate for daily life and get as many kids to pass as you can. Whatever it takes, whatever else you have to set aside, I'm afraid that's what you'll have to do.

Both shrug. They exit.

*   *   *

It is significant that the initial push toward minimum competency testing came primarily from outside the education field (Pipho 1979a). Educators by and large have been against the idea, although a few have broken ranks. It is probably fair to say that most educators see minimum competency testing as more of a problem than a solution.

Some of the advocates, though lacking professional credentials and experience in education, have enough understanding of what schooling involves to qualify at least as dedicated amateurs—Admiral Rickover, for example, to whom I shall return shortly. Others who came to the issue more recently may not know enough about the realities of education to pass practical judgment, though they share a genuine sense of alarm that the schools may be failing. No doubt many state legislators are in this category. Probably still other people have joined the testing movement for political or economic gain, with little interest otherwise. There are always quacks and charlatans lurking at the school yard fence ready to take advantage of sudden changes in the flow of educational funds and power.

In education, however, ignorance is no bar to opinion. It has been our tradition for centuries that education is properly everyone's business. In a democratic society everyone, informed or not, has the right to be heard, and all the more so on issues that touch people so close to home. And even a doctorate in education, unfortunately, gives no assurance of wisdom. The American insistence on local control of education, in contrast to the practice in many other nations, simply reflects a widely held conviction that individual citizens should be empowered to influence the course of education in their own localities.

On the other hand, problems always seem simpler from a distance. Every cabdriver in Washington seems to know exactly what to do about inflation and unemployment, and most will address themselves to pedagogy as well. The only people without ready solutions, it appears, are those who best understand the problems.

Thus, many educators remain uneasy about minimum competency testing, even though the public, through its elected representatives, has spoken out in favor of competency tests. The reasons educators put forth for their reservations make up a large part of this book. Put briefly, however, much of the debate comes down to a discrepancy between public and professional views of education. And nowhere does the discrepancy become clearer than in picking standards, that is, in choosing competencies to be tested and in specifying minimum levels of attainment.

Indeed, the word *standards* is itself part of the problem. It has a way of shifting its meaning in midthought. In one sense, "standards" connotes quality generally, as in, "She is a person of high standards." In another sense, the same word refers to methods for assessing quality: "There are no standards for judging a wholly new art form." The two meanings are very different. Confusion between them has exacerbated the present tug-of-war between educators and others who take an interest in education.

In 1977, Admiral Hyman Rickover, a long-time critic of what he calls the "educational establishment," confused these meanings of the word *standards* in testimony before a Senate subcommittee. The admiral's remarks were reprinted nationally, enjoyed wide discussion in the media, and may have contributed to the surge in minimum competency testing in the two years that followed.

Rickover opened with his view of education's failings in recent years, based on declining test scores and his own informal impressions. He moved on to the familiar list of causes: grade inflation, low demands on students, insufficient parental confidence and interest, television, incompetent teachers, and, especially, stonewalling by the educational establishment. Then came his proposed remedy:

> I recommend, Mr. Chairman, that you and perhaps your counterpart in the House of Representatives appoint a panel of nationally prominent persons in representative walks of life to develop national scholastic standards.
>
> The standards should consist of specific minimum compe-

tency requirements for various levels—second grade, fourth grade, sixth grade, and so on. In addition, there should be a formal system of tests to show not only the relative standing of students and schools against national norms, but also whether students meet the minimum competency requirements. Thus a yardstick would be provided to measure academic performance—a means of assessing achievement of individual students, effectiveness of teachers, and overall academic attainment of schools. Summaries of test results by school, district, and state would enable parents and educators to measure where their schools stand relative to the national standards and to other schools in the country. For the first time, parents would have a means to hold teachers and schools accountable for the quality of their work.[2]

There is a subtle sidestep in Rickover's argument, one that also appears in many other discussions. Rickover's goal is improved education, especially in the three Rs. What that will take, he says, is demanding curriculum, qualified teachers, and hard work from students. No news there. But Rickover does not tell us how to bring about these improvements in the current political and economic environment. That is, he offers no suggestions on how to raise standards. Instead, he urges standards of a different sort: tests that might measure whether improvement takes place but which cannot, by themselves, achieve it. In Alan Watts's memorable phrase, it is eating the menu instead of the dinner.

The confusion among meanings makes it uncouth to criticize tests at all, when competency standards are at stake. Any negative remark on the tests is likely to be construed as an attack on quality, the quality that the tests are supposed to measure. Paul Houts observed this problem at a conference during a wide-ranging discussion of minimum competency:

> Those advancing the cause of minimum competency requirements perceived any attack on such requirements as an attack on standards, if not competency. . . . In turn, those opposing the competency tests were forced to argue against measures designed to ensure competency while not rejecting competency as a valid goal of the schools (Houts 1979, p. 13).

Those in favor of competency tests, in other words, hold the moral high ground and defend it under the banner of "standards." Indeed, the word carries a powerful emotional charge. Talk of "high standards" evokes a sense of ambition and achievement, inspiring trust in the people who profess to live by such standards.

Thus, when Rickover and others imply that the schools are utterly without standards, the accusation hits hard. Yet the charge is untrue. Schools have always had standards. To be sure, these standards cover the spectrum from mediocrity to excellence, according to local resources and circumstances, and they are seldom expressed numerically. But standards have to reflect prevailing conditions and require a certain degree of flexibility. Without flexibility they can only result in pointless frustration among poorer students and needless laxity among the better ones (Tyler 1979*b*, p. 28).

This is why the schools do not have what Rickover seeks: a national homogenization of standards coupled with a national mechanism to see where those standards are being met. To lack these, however, is a very different thing from operating with no standards at all.

The elusive meaning of standards leads to a further problem. In the sense of goals, standards are something to strive after; but they need not be attained in every case. "A man's reach must exceed his grasp," said Browning, to which Jerrold Zacharias adds, "but not by too much." Standards, which should inspire people to greater accomplishment, cannot serve that purpose if they fall too easily within reach.

When the word *standards* comes to mean a test, the criteria for success are different. Then almost everyone must pass or the schools will have failed those who do not. Standard-as-goal can be demanding; standard-as-test must be attainable by all. As a result, inevitably, the translation of standards into tests means that the standards must decline so as to fall within reach. In a minimum competency environment, students who once might have strived for excellence soon come to understand that mediocrity is enough. Having met the prevailing standards, they have little incentive to go further.

Minimum competency, in short, is not likely to raise standards as its advocates claim. Rather, it changes the meaning of standards and, in so doing, lowers them considerably. A Denver senior commenting on his own test put it succinctly. "If you can't pass that," he said, "you have the IQ of an artichoke" (Frahm and Covington 1979, p. 8). He may be right; fewer than 2 percent of the Denver graduating class are denied diplomas each year (Frahm and Covington 1979, p. 16). Either the people in Denver know something the rest of us do not—maybe it's the thin air—or their standards are not so high after all.

To put the issue a little differently, standards take on different meanings according to whether they apply to groups or individuals. In a particular school with high standards, not every student need excel, even though the school demands much of its students as a group. The school can succeed even if some of its students do not. Applying the same standards to individuals, however, changes the situation from group success to many individual failures. The only alternative, again, is to lower the standards until most individuals succeed. But then the school as a whole becomes a failure. There is no way to succeed on both counts, simply because individuals are so different in their capabilities.

The rhetoric on standards that peppers discussions of minimum competency testing carries a forceful ring. But when the rhetoric changes to practice, the ring becomes a dull thud. The effort to establish uniform standards can only bring discouragement to the large majority of students and their teachers.

An analogy, though farfetched, may help to illustrate some of the problems in setting meaningful standards. Suppose that a state legislature were concerned about the quality of health among its constituents. Many physicians, it hears, are not making sufficient efforts to keep their patients at the necessary minimum standards of well-being. Accordingly, the legislature passes a law. Henceforth, a physician must examine all of his patients every year to be sure they are healthy. That way, the reasoning goes, people who need help can be identified in time to correct their problems. No sick people will be able to slip through the system unnoticed, except those with no doctor at all. And if any physicians are not doing their jobs, that fact will come to light when too many of their patients fail the exams.

Such a law might be superficially attractive, until one thinks about implementing it. Then it becomes a nightmare. The central questions are what to include in the examination, and what operational criteria should represent minimum standards of health.

It is clear that lay people cannot make these decisions. A legislature might specify examination of, say, the circulatory system, the nervous system, and a vague range of chemistries; but translating these guidelines into a precise examination can only be done by professionals.

The criteria chosen will determine directly who emerges as sick or healthy. If the standards are the textbook ideals of human functioning, a large proportion of the population will fail them, including many who are in no immediate danger of serious illness. The consequence will be a dramatic and unnecessary increase in the cost of medical care. If, on the other hand, the standards are so low as to include people who can barely clamber out of bed, the plan loses most of its practical value. Sick people will stay sick.

The final criteria will have to be the product of compromise and as such will probably rest as much on economic and political considerations as on medical wisdom. In practice, it will likely be impossible to find a uniform set of standards that can distinguish wholesale between those who need treatment and those who do not. More likely, the standards will represent a balance between the public's idealized image of good health, on the high side, and the number of people that the public is willing to accept labeled as ill, on the low.

There is also the question of who will tend to the sick while doctors are tied up examining people who mostly don't need it. One solution is to subcontract the task to national examining companies, though some states will no doubt prefer to establish their own procedures. The examining companies, for their part, can be expected to publish alarming data on the decline in health, thus fostering a demand for legislation that will require their services.

No matter who does the examining, physicians will have little incentive to work with patients who either come well below the standard or far surpass it. Instead, a doctor will make his reputation, and perhaps his greatest income, with people who are a little below the standard by applying only enough treatment to bring them just above it. Such "specialization" will produce an impressive record of success in the state's files, which may be useful if the state ever imposes accountability as part of the medical relicensing procedure. A doctor will then be threatening his own future if he spends time reassuring a pregnant woman or patiently explaining to a man terminally ill with cancer what his options are. It will be far more productive to prescribe for otherwise healthy people with merely slight defects in their lab results.

We can pursue the analogy further by presenting official certificates of health to people who pass their examinations. Of course, employers will insist on seeing these because, on the whole, healthy workers can be expected to show up for work more often and produce more. In most cases, health standards for the certificate will bear no particular relation to the stamina required for a particular job. But that will quickly become irrelevant. Few employers will trouble to examine candidates themselves when they can simply look at a state certificate. People who have no certificate, for whatever reason, will soon find themselves unemployable.

Certain parts of the population will find it harder than others to obtain their certificates. Among some minority groups, for example, long-standing poverty will have contributed to chronic malnutrition and to lack of adequate medical care in the past. Consequently, a disproportionate number may have the stigma of lacking a health certificate and therefore find themselves unemployable, even for jobs they could easily handle. No doubt there will be lawsuits claiming that the examinations are discriminatory in their effects and so should be banned. Advocates, in the meantime, will argue that maintaining the examinations is the best way to keep incentives for good health among all people, minorities included.

Just as in the medical analogy, most of the problems in minimum competency testing come to rest, in one way or another, on the notion of fixed and uniform standards. The question of standards, in fact, can help to determine whether the basic idea of minimum competency makes sense in the first place. To be at all realistic, competency standards must meet three conditions: (1) the public must accept the standards as representing the satisfactory outcome of a high school education; (2) employers must find them a useful index for selecting incoming workers; and (3) the schools must be able to achieve them for an acceptable number of students without having to discard other, equally important goals. If no such standards are possible, then the minimum competency movement is all but doomed from the outset.

And indeed, standards and requirements meeting these three conditions have proved difficult to find in practice. Walt Haney and George Madaus (1979*a,* p. 32) report that it is easier to reach agreement on general areas of competence than it is to specify precise minimum cutoffs within those areas.

Every state involved in competency testing looks at reading, and nearly all assess computation and writing as well. A few states go beyond the three Rs to examine, in addition, such topics as consumer economics, social studies, science, government, spelling, listening, problem solving, and free enterprise (Pipho 1979*b*). In some states, it seems, the method for achieving consensus is simply to include every subject that anyone suggests. The decisions, in any event, typically come more from political than pedagogic concerns (Haney and Madaus 1979*a,* p. 32).

The setting of numerical requirements within the academic areas is subject to pressures from both politics and pedagogy. "On the political side, a standard that is so high that many students fail reflects poorly upon the school for the ill preparation of students. Yet if the standard is set low, patrons can complain that the school is not rigorous in its demands for quality. One teacher representative described this dilemma as a 'no win' situation" (Miller 1978, p. 15). I would add that the dilemma stems once again from different uses of the word *standards.*

Looked at another way, the same tension reflects a need to accommodate not only what students should know, but also what the schools think they can teach (Baratz 1979, p. 39). Gene Glass of the University of Colorado goes so far as to argue that "every attempt to derive a criterion score [for example, to define minimum competency] is either blatantly arbitrary or derives from a set of arbitrary premises" (quoted in Haney and Madaus 1978*a,* p. 466).

The arbitrary nature of the standards goes beyond mere caprice, for the very meaning of minimum competency is hard to pin down (Haney and Madaus 1978*a,* p. 465). At stake are some of education's most fundamental assumptions. People charged with designing the tests find themselves forced to confront nothing less than the question of what societal purposes the schools are supposed to fulfill. This is a surprising depth of inquiry for what seems, on the surface, to be a straightforward task of establishing minimum competencies. The need arises from the discrepant views of education held by those who launched minimum competency testing in the first place and by those who must now implement it.

For example, test authors must decide whether to test "school skills," "life skills," or some proportion of each. The testing controversy has uncovered a belief among many noneducators that schools teach, or should teach, skills that people need in ordinary adult life. This has not been a primary goal of education until recently, except for the poorest students. What the schools do teach is a set of higher order skills (so-called) for acquiring whatever further skills students may need later on.

Reading is one example of a skill that can serve many purposes. What do people actually read in "adult life"? The most read magazine seems to be *TV Guide*; the most read newspaper, the *New York Daily News*; and the most read book, the Bible. With these facts, we can construct a sort of syllogism.

Major premise: Schools should teach children to read for adult life.

Minor premise: Adults read *TV Guide,* etc.

Conclusion: Schools should teach children to read *TV Guide.*

No school currently uses *TV Guide* in its curriculum, at least none that I know of. Considering that television is widely regarded as responsible for many of the schools' problems, keeping program listings in the classroom would be too much like consorting with the enemy. But the materials that schools do use ought to prepare a student for *TV Guide,* and for almost any other nontechnical written matter. From its very beginning, education has relied on the leverage of generality: Teach the general ability and all the more specific skills that flow from it will thereby be available.

Training, as distinct from education, takes a much more direct approach. Indeed, the minimum competency movement seems to be pushing schools toward a model long familiar in military and industrial training. Take, for example, the task of teaching a man to operate a hoist that lifts heavy equipment. One method is to begin with the physics of the hoist: conservation of energy, its application in mechanical advantage, electrical propulsion, the arrangement of motor and machinery that makes this particular hoist work, and finally, the fact that the green button sends the hoist up, and the red button brings it back down. An industrial trainer, of course, would not teach that way. Instead he would just point to the buttons in turn, saying, "Up. Down." Next, he would test the operator's skills at pushing the two buttons and then leave. The first approach might take a couple of years; the second, a couple of minutes.

There are powerful arguments for teaching a push-button form of reading in school. Such a movement has made inroads on education periodically, starting just before World War I (Callahan 1962), and appearing most recently during the brief skirmish with performance contracting in the early 1970s. The principle of the movement is to define precisely the outcome sought and to move directly toward that outcome with as few intervening stages as possible.

The trend toward teaching "life skills," emerging as part of the minimum competency movement — reading want ads, balancing check books, and similar practical tasks — is the current expression of the same school of pedagogy. This time push-button pedagogy takes root where the meaning of "standards" changes from goals to tests. The goal of teaching children the reading skills they will need as adults has been the unchallenged, primary goal of formal education ever since somebody found a way to make marks stand for sounds. To measure those skills, however, requires something to read. A test has to be very specific. When the test focuses on adult needs, and when those in turn are set at the lowest possible common denominator, the measure of success becomes, not reading in general, but reading want ads. With that, a curriculum of want ads becomes almost inevitable.

Reading want ads and the like is just the outcome that some advocates of minimum competency testing are seeking. Teaching about want ads has a hardheaded and businesslike flavor: Never mind the fancy stuff; just teach the kids what they need. Many people assume that industry endorses this view, seeking recruits who can accurately read assembly instructions even if they don't know a simile from a metaphor. Some educators think that industry's motives are economic: the reduction of expenses in training employees. A few go as far as to espouse a conspiracy theory in which industry and its political allies snipe at the best interests of children from the grassy knoll of the state legislature.

With a little more ingenuity, truly paranoid fantasies can be developed. Sherwood Kohn set tongue firmly in cheek to sketch this fascinating scenario, here slightly condensed with Kohn's permission:

> A giant, multinational corporation has assessed world socioeconomic trends and projected that technological developments offer them two options for the future. They can apply their enormous research and development potential in the service of mankind, or they can use their power to control a largely benighted and subservient population for the purpose of building a world wherein they rule "in the interest" of the masses. They decide on the latter course.
>
> For this purpose, they need institute no new controls. But they must increasingly deny the general populace access to information. They must dehumanize people; they must sort them carefully into the rulers and the ruled; they must withhold education or restrict it severely; and they must make education, access to data, and critical thought the exclusive province of the ruling class. Fortunately, even the sorting mechanisms—the three or four national testing firms—are already in place. It remains only for these firms to be consolidated and for a single set

of standardized tests to be mandated by federal law.

In fact, as the story opens, the testing firms have just finished telling the people that their standardized reading, writing, and computing skill scores are declining, and that they must approve a nationwide program of minimum competency education. The multinational corporation expects that once the program is established, schools will narrow their curricula until all education is reduced to a set of basic mechanical skills. Critical thinking, not to mention the broad range of humanistic studies, will disappear entirely from the public schools (Kohn 1979, p. 47).

Many concerned educators share Kohn's fears of the outcome he warns against. But there is no evidence to speak of that either industry or the military—another conspirator, in some versions—plays any important role in fostering the minimum competency movement. Among the movement's advocates, all the same, are those who applaud the shift from broad educational aims to more specific, practically oriented skills.

Despite all the debate over school skills versus life skills, test items tend to blur the distinction anyway. Multiple choice is a highly restrictive medium. Regardless of the input, the items testing life skills and school skills come out looking very much the same.

In mathematics, for example, Educational Testing Service offers the following as a "real life task":

A job pays $6.50 per hour with time-and-a-half for overtime. If you work 40 regular hours and 8 overtime hours at that job, how much would you earn?

(A) $360 (B) $312 (C) $338 (D) $468

(quoted in Southeastern Public Education Program 1978, p. 12)

The solution of such a problem is not a real life task at all. It is entirely a school skill, under the heading of "word problems." The question looks like something out of a textbook. Rarely does real experience provide situations with all the information so tidily laid out; rarely is it worthwhile to perform such calculations longhand; and rarely does anyone need an answer so precise as to distinguish among the first three answers given. In school, though, such artificialities are commonplace. The problem, in fact, bears about the same relationship to the corresponding real situation as a formal portrait does to the person pictured: flat, devoid of depth and motion, and with every hair in place.

Much the same is true of minimum competency items in general, even those little writing exercises in which the student must pretend to be a mythical person applying for a mythical job. There, too, the needed information appears in neat rows—and again, the niceties of form are all-important. Real life is too big and too messy for a classroom test. Confusing its pale reflection on paper with "real life tasks" calls to mind Edwin F. Taylor's (1977*a*) cynical remark about "the looking-glass world of testing" that imposes on students its own special fantasy of real life.

All the same, a change in educational goals toward more practically oriented skills does have some advantages. It may well render a greater proportion of high school graduates able to cope with the mechanics of daily life. At the same time, however, such a change will just as certainly reduce the proportion of graduates who are capable of abstract and original thought, or at least who have enough intellectual inventory to make their thinking effective. There will be more people competent as hoist operators, perhaps, but fewer who can deduce the operation of an unfamiliar hoist. Fewer still will be able to devise a new and better one.

Often heard is the counterargument that "minimum competency" means what it says. It does not mean the maximum or even necessarily the average. Thus, children capable of more advanced work should be encouraged to pursue it, just as they have been encouraged in the past.

As a group, educators have responded skeptically to this defense. For reasons I shall enumerate in the following chapter, the schools feel that they are under enormous pressure to deliver the greatest possible number of minimally competent students—

and find themselves unable, at the same time, to fully meet the needs of students far above that level, or those far below it. Putting full effort into all kinds of goals simultaneously is impossible in practice. A great many students may still achieve well beyond the minimum, but probably not to the extent that they could if the pressures of minimum competency were absent from the educational system.

These issues have implications far beyond the schoolhouse. They speak ultimately to the kind of society we wish to have when today's students are in charge. For example, we have seen both elitism and respect for "progress" come into disrepute over the past decade or two. It is fortunate that these notions declined together, for progress has always been an elitist pursuit: Though calling on the efforts of many, progress typically depends on a kind of intellectual spark that very few in each generation are able to provide. One long-term effect of the competency movement may be to reduce further the number of exceptionally competent people, though we cannot be sure of that until some time in the next millennium.

For a society so beset with genuinely tough problems as ours is, it seems shortsighted to brush aside the youngest and brightest in our midst so that their classmates can learn to solve artificial word problems about overtime pay. Or perhaps, as another cynic has said, we expect bright children to get an education in spite of their schooling.

The present arrangements for arriving at educational standards are haphazard, but at least until recently they have served us well. If something has come unstuck in the past few years, prudence would advise tapping it back into place gently so as not to disturb the surrounding social machinery whose operation we poorly understand. Instead, we are attacking the educational system with a sledge and might even be hammering on the wrong part of the machine.

To say, "Certain skills are absolutely basic for everyone" amounts to a history-defying proposition of social philosophy. The statement reflects a particular view of society and of the individual's role in it, a view whose validity is far from certain. We might just as easily imagine societies in which that statement is completely wrong. Those would include, in fact, just about every society throughout history but our own, and many would say that ours belongs on the list too. Even if the statement is true for the United States in the 1980s — and perhaps it is, for sufficiently limited skills — it needs a great deal more thoughtful qualification than any state legislature has yet bestowed upon it. This premise of the minimum competency movement assumes that the social engineering on which the movement rests is a reliable science. As sciences go, however, that particular one lends itself to mistakes that are disastrously expensive, in terms of both money and people's lives.

Furthermore, to maintain that a roomful of people can decide, for everyone else, what those absolutely necessary skills are can only be called arrogant. Nor does it help much to make that roomful "broadly representative," although no one nowadays would think of making it otherwise. Everyone who has tried to convene a group according to demographic requirements knows the dilemma: either some good people must be left out, because they are the wrong color, make the wrong amount of money, or come from the same place as too many other good people; or the group becomes unmanageably large in order to maintain the required proportions.

The greater the divergence of opinions, moreover, the greater the need for political compromise in the group. It is necessary to hear all sides. But the effort to accommodate all sides is likely to produce results that satisfy no one, least of all the people whose lives will be affected. Too often, the product of compromise is ambiguity and vagueness, which in practice may translate to unpredictable and unreasonable requirements.

Whatever the process for determining educational standards, the standards that emerge will override a centuries-old evolution of trial and error in education, will bear the full force of the law, and will act to freeze society's options by predetermining its people's abilities. Naming those standards is a frightening task, one safely entrusted only to men and women of the greatest courage and wisdom. Those standards, in the end, will determine whether minimum competency testing serves society well or undermines us all.

Notes

1. See Jencks 1978.
2. U.S., Congress, Senate, Committee on Labor and Human Resources, Subcommittee on Education, Arts, and Humanities, *Quality of Education, Hearings before a Subcommittee of the Senate Committee on Labor and Human Resources,* 95th Cong., 1st sess., 1977, p. 3.

4

Effects of Minimum Competency Testing on Curriculum

T ests exert an enormous impact on curriculum. We take that fact for granted nowadays. With the quality of educators' work increasingly equated with test scores, the people who plan curriculum simply must suit their product to the tests. The national goal in education has become high test scores, and anyone who disagrees publicly with that goal will have trouble keeping a job in state or local education.

It does seem backward, though, that curriculum is influenced by tests. After all, curriculum is what we teach and how we teach it — the very essence of education. Tests are only devices to measure the outcome of curriculum. One might as well try to move a car by twisting the speedometer needle. In this view, it would make more sense to plan the curriculum first, based not on tests, but on what children need to know and are capable of learning.

These quaint ideas actually had some currency in the last century. Then, the only tests in school were teacher-made quizzes and examinations. The change first began in the high schools, when the Educational Testing Service began publishing the nationally uniform SAT soon after 1900. In the following decades, the proliferation of standardized, widely distributed achievement tests for the lower grades pushed the test makers' influence into elementary school. The imposition of large-scale tests from outside the school building and district left educators little choice but to adjust their curricula accordingly.

The SAT and the commercial achievement tests do not affect curriculum unilaterally, however. The authors of the tests, for the most part, try to devise items based on what they believe most schools are teaching. The result has been a long-standing, uneasy equilibrium between the content of these tests and curriculum.[1]

Minimum competency tests have now upset that equilibrium. Again, the tests come from outside the curriculum process, but there is no need for the authors to reflect current teaching at all. On the contrary, the test is typically mandated as a result of frustration with current curricula. The express aim is often to alter curricula in directions chosen by those who institute the tests, most often in the direction of "basic skills." And educators have little choice but to comply. With public attention on the test results, with the possibility of students failing to receive diplomas, and with the risk of lawsuits from students who fail (see Chapter 7), curriculum designers and classroom teachers are pressured to "teach to the test." Minimum competency tests, in practice, control much of the curriculum in their subject areas.

Even more than their teachers, students know that the test is what matters most. "Are we responsible for this on the test?" is the student's way of asking, "Is this worth my trouble to learn?" When the answer is no, attention is turned off as if by the flick of a switch.

There is a worthwhile lesson in Jerrold Zacharias's story of how he himself first came to appreciate the importance of tests. He was then still at the Massachusetts Institute of Technology as institute professor emeritus of physics, before his move to Education Development Center. With a few of his colleagues, Zacharias was on a committee to recommend changes in MIT's undergraduate program. The group resolved, as a first step, to find out exactly what the undergraduates were then learning. And so they sat in on classes, studied the text materials in detail, and worked alongside students in the laboratories. Their months of work yielded an exact specification of course content.

Eventually the time came for final exams. Most finals at MIT in those days were three-hour ordeals covering the entire semester. Zacharias and his friends duly received copies of the exams—and had a rude shock. There, laid out in tidy question form, was all of the information they had acquired so laboriously on their own. What were students expected to learn? The answers to the questions on the tests. And as almost everyone passed routinely, that was, in fact, what students were learning. The tests were the real curriculum.

Students, of course, had reached the same conclusion generations earlier. That is why old exams are such popular study aids. What is important to know in this course? Whatever was on last year's exam!

Zacharias—who, incidentally, left a career as a world famous experimental physicist in 1956 to spend the next quarter century developing precollege curriculum[2]—understood the implications. If the "real curriculum" is the test, then tests provide a convenient lever for curriculum change. The tests are curricula writ small, so that altering a handful of test questions can have an enormously magnified effect on curricular practice, which must follow along. "Let me write a nation's tests," Zacharias used to say, "and let who will, write its poetry." That is also the governing principle of the minimum competency movement, though its advocates seem not to care whether the poetry gets written at all.

In recent years, Zacharias has expanded his ideas beyond curriculum and tests to designate the national efforts in education, taken as a whole, as a "system." Nowadays systems terminology is very much in vogue for everything from cameras to psychotherapy. But as a physicist, Zacharias uses the term in a stricter sense than most: A system is a collection of elements so interrelated that a change in any one of them is liable to change any of the others. He and Saville Davis, formerly managing editor of the *Christian Science Monitor,* have developed a systems theory of education in considerable detail in a forthcoming book. The elements of their system involve aspects of education as diverse as the federal government, textbooks, colleges of education, and of course, tests.

Their theory has considerable appeal. I will mention just one example of its application: an explanation of why most educational reforms in the past century have failed. The educational system, they argue, tends toward equilibrium by absorbing change, much as physiological systems in the body absorb attempts to change their equilibria. To be effective, then, lasting educational change would require adjustment of many parts of the system at the same time, making all the adjustments consistent with the desired outcome. The system as a whole, not just a few of its parts, must be tuned to the new equilibrium. It will be interesting to see whether minimum competency testing, which gives a sudden wrench to one part of the system and leaves the rest to follow, will confirm their theory by leaving the system in a new equilibrium that accommodates the change with the least possible disruption.

The theory predicts, nonetheless, that the imposition of change on one element will have abrupt effects elsewhere as the system shifts to adjust. That is part of the absorptive process. The theory does not say just what those effects will be in the case of minimum competency testing, but some are not hard to foresee.

The preceding chapter touched on some of the impact that minimum competency will likely have on schooling, particularly on reading. We can summarize this impact in a sentence: Schools will teach to the tests. They have to. Society has laid down two simple instructions to the schools. One is ancient; the other, very recent.

1. (ancient) You must do a good job of educating.

2. (modern) Doing a good job means enabling many students to pass the minimum competency tests.

Both commands apply simultaneously. There can be only one intelligent response: Orient the curriculum around the tests. And as the tests are likely to be trivial in most cases—the multiple-choice format encourages that—curriculum must become trivial also. That is an overstatement, of course, but inevitably the pressure on curriculum will encourage teaching easily testable "bits" of knowledge.

Teachers have been among the first to catch on. Ralph Tyler, a prominent educator who chaired a panel to evaluate the

Florida accountability program, reports in dismay that "some of the teachers [in Florida] actually believed that the law now required them to narrow the curriculum to those minimum competencies. . . . [M]any teachers interpreted the emphasis on basic skills to mean that they must devote most of their attention to routine drill" (Tyler 1979*a,* p. 29). The teachers were largely right. True, the law does not call for a narrow curriculum in so many words. But in setting up a measure of curriculum based on narrow tests, the law does indirectly narrow the curriculum exactly as the teachers believed.

Even so, the minimum competency movement is hardly a new pressure on curriculum. Similar trends have recurred throughout the century and probably earlier as well. The present curricular shifts, in fact, began long before any state, except possibly Oregon, had mandated competency testing. The early 1970s saw a banner reading "back to basics" hoisted over the three Rs. Minimum competency is the older back-to-basics movement written into state law.

Nor did back-to-basics spring from nowhere. According to Walt Haney and George Madaus, both it and minimum competency are aspects of "a backlash against what columnist James J. Kilpatrick calls 'funsie-wunsie open education'" (Haney and Madaus 1979*c,* p. 16). The popular press seems to agree and sometimes ties minimum competency to a populist-style parents' revolt against the damages thought to result from the open education of the 1960s.

The truth is not that simple, however. "Open education" was not a single, uniform program, but rather a diverse collection; it included an amazing variety of educational practices. Many worked out well, though the failures had far more press coverage. Probably the best-known failure was the "new math," to which I shall return later in this chapter. Yet the new math, strictly speaking, was not part of the open education movement at all and only happened to coincide with it historically.

Justifiably or not, nevertheless, the collapse of open education is an important factor in the widespread acceptance of minimum competency. Accordingly, a brief historical account of open education may help to show why minimum competency found such a welcome reception and offers some insight into the kinds of curriculum likely to spring from the testing programs.

Originally, the expression "open education" referred to a style of classroom management in which students had considerable freedom in choosing their activities from hour to hour. With the freedom came a need for changes in the physical layout of the classroom itself. "Activity centers" replaced fixed desks and chairs, making it easier for students to switch from one type of work to another. "Hands-on activities" proliferated because they functioned well with the small groups of students studying independently at each center.

Changes in teaching technique also brought changes in what was taught. The traditional rote-and-drill approach to the three Rs gave way to broader explorations of a variety of topics that, until then, had not played any significant role in elementary education. It also became practical to combine topics of study with activities that children found highly motivating. To take just one example, some elementary students explored the nineteenth-century New England whaling industry through a variety of written and hands-on materials and audiovisuals. In the process, they acquired a good deal of information about geography, history, economics, ecology, technology change — and even literature, by reading excerpts from *Moby Dick* in a context that made sense. A good deal of reading was involved, and in some classrooms, writing and arithmetic as well. Most important, the whole enterprise played to children's interest in ships and animals, encouraging a level of involvement seldom seen in "traditional" classrooms.

What went wrong? The answer would require a book in itself, for there is still not much agreement on what the major problems were. We can, however, identify three with reasonable certainty.

1. Open education required teachers who were sympathetic to that method of teaching and trained to use it. (The same is true, of course, of every other method.) Many school districts imposed open education on teachers who were unprepared, and the results were sometimes disastrous.

2. When the decline in SAT scores became widely known,

many authors noted that the onset of the decline corresponded roughly with the introduction of open education. There is now some evidence otherwise, but at the time it was easy to conclude that open education was to blame for the drop in scores.

3. Two programs popularly associated with open education failed conspicuously, one pedagogically and one politically. The first, the new math, had little to do with open education, but it helped to bring the demise of open education by association. The second program, Education Development Center's *Man: A Course of Study* (MACOS), was a tremendous success in the classroom. But its hundreds of pages and hours of film included one or two very brief scenes that offended some parents. (For example, one film sequence showed a Netsilik Eskimo seal hunt in which the hunter's child ate the eye of a seal.) MACOS became a cause of the political Right in some parts of the country, complete with house-to-house petitions. It was debated on the floor of the House of Representatives, where the sponsor of the program, the National Science Foundation, received negative attention. The controversy helped to shift the public mood (and congressional appropriations) away from open education, as if these isolated problems had somehow infected the whole movement.

The reaction to newspaper coverage of these problems came very quickly. *Reader's Digest* and other conservative publishers ran horror stories of children running amok in the classroom. Use of open education, widespread at the time, dropped precipitously over two or three years. The retreat from open education required a positive-sounding slogan and "back-to-basics" was it. Innovative educators tried to redefine "basics" in terms of their own goals, hoping to co-opt the movement — or at least the slogan. But the tactic came to nothing when the minimum competency tests defined once and for all what "basic" really means, i.e., certain subskills in reading, writing, and arithmetic, occasionally dressed up as real-life problems. The tests were supposed to prevent, in the future, the harms open education had wrought in the past. And with that, the open education movement — indeed, two exciting decades of educational improvement — was over.

Unfortunately, the quick retreat seems to have solved no problems. Test scores are still declining, though occasional data give score watchers some cause for hope. Students do not seem to be reading and writing appreciably better, despite the enormous time and effort now devoted to basic skills.

One might even suggest — very cautiously, from behind a stack of purple drill sheets — that perhaps open education and other innovations were not the real culprits after all. Maybe the real problems are much tougher — issues like changing demographics, shifting attitudes about individual effort, reluctance to impose hard work on children, parental apathy, and even growing questions of whether education actually benefits people in the end. Whichever view of why test scores are declining is correct, minimum competency cannot be much of a solution unless we first know what the problems are.

Open education brought valuable learning experiences into the classroom, often with great success. Many children not only learned to read and write, but also discovered firsthand what reading and writing are for. There can be no better way to promote learning than to make it intrinsically worthwhile, and open education did that. It was bad enough that back-to-basics put the emphasis exclusively on skills, at the expense of teaching how to use them in pursuit of one's own interests. Now, minimum competency is cutting back even further, making the isolated skills even more important than ever. "Why do I have to learn this?" asks the child. The teacher now has a final reply: "Because the law says you have to."

Open education was both an approach to curricular content and a method for teaching it. Back-to-basics likewise stresses specific content and also has a teaching method: the "traditional" classroom techniques that have predominated for most of this century. Minimum competency, too, has its content — the skills needed to pass the tests — but so far has lacked a method specifically suited to its needs.

As the movement becomes further entrenched, educators will be casting about for teaching methods that offer consistent performance on the tests. Education is a fad-ridden business anyway; but added pressure from the tests may promote even more than usual the tendency to grasp uncritically at anything with promise.

To gain special favor in the minimum competency environment, a pedagogy would have to make at least three major claims: first, that it succeeds with the vast majority of children; second, that it has sufficient flexibility to accommodate the minor differences among state competency laws; and third, that it functions well in ordinary classrooms with ordinary teachers and without much added expense. A fourth helpful characteristic would be suitability to the fragmentation of knowledge that goes along with multiple-choice tests.

As it happens, there is an emerging pedagogy that makes the first three claims, and to which the fourth may apply also. It is called "learning for mastery," or, in the alphabet soup of educationese, LFM. Dating originally from the mid-1960s, LFM has grown remarkably over the last few years. Though its advocates have not suggested any special appropriateness to minimum competency, as far as I know, it seems likely that LFM or something like it will become the preferred teaching method in many of the minimum competency states. A brief look at the strengths and failings of LFM may thus provide a small, clouded glimpse into the immediate future of American education.

LFM derives from the work of Benjamin Bloom, who maintains as a first principle that all children are created equal: "Each student may be helped to learn a particular subject to the same degree, level of competence, and even in approximately the same amount of time" (quoted in Glickman 1979). In particular, Bloom asserts that classifying children as slow, average, or fast learners is a myth — that 95 percent of the population are equally capable of learning (Glickman 1979). These claims attempt to overturn decades of work in child development, including virtually all of the work on children's "stages" of development by Piaget and others. Bloom's assertion has special appeal to people who hope to show a 95 percent success rate on their state tests.

LFM advocates seem to say, moreover, that a belief in more

traditional theories of child development actually holds children back:

> Our firm conclusion after 16 years of working with thousands of teachers is that many unwittingly retard their children's learning by rationalizing more practice and a slower pace than is required. . . . [T]he one factor that continues to explain LFM success appears to be this same antidote to teacher-caused retardation—the fact that mastery points [objectives] are defined and demonstrated, causing a forward motion through a continuum leading to more learning in a given amount of time (Hyman and Cohen 1979, p. 106).

A second key element of LFM is "time on task," the percentage of time that students actually participate in learning. (The percentage of time on task is now more scientifically termed the "P Ratio.") Research has long shown the obvious, that students will learn more if they spend more time at it; and classrooms using LFM apparently do achieve higher P Ratios than traditional classrooms.

Hyman and Cohen list seven techniques for keeping the P Ratio high. The following is, I hasten to add, a direct quote:

> a. Define instructional objectives behaviorally so that learner and teacher know exactly where they are, where they are going, and where they have been.

> b. Go directly to the defined behavior—that is, direct teaching of the behavior or "attitude" sought rather than "building to it" or around it.

> c. Provide immediate feedback to all learner responses. The more immediate the feedback, the more efficient the learning.

> d. Rig the level of instruction so that feedback is maximally positive. Success breeds success and lots of warm fuzzies too.

> e. Modularize learning by cutting down the bites to small, self-contained nibbles. Closure is the most potent of all positive feedback techniques. The smaller the bite, the more immediate the closure.

> f. Control the stimulus so we know exactly what the learner is responding to. That is a major problem in commercially published materials.

g. Reinforce by positive feedback the learner's critical response. The critical response is the one that responds to the appropriate stimulus defined precisely by the instructional objective (Hyman and Cohen 1979, p. 106).

This approach calls to mind not education in any traditional sense, but training in the military or industrial style, "lots of warm fuzzies" notwithstanding. (Warm fuzzies, I suppose, are good feelings about schoolwork, which are important whatever they are called. Good feelings about school are probably the single most important factor in student motivation.) The LFM approach is also reminiscent of computer-aided instruction (CAI), or, rather, the relatively primitive form of CAI that enjoyed brief popularity in the 1960s.

More generally, the method has a decidedly behavioristic flavor. Advocates refer to "stimulus" and "reinforcement," key words in the behaviorist vocabulary. There is considerable emphasis on what the behaviorists call reinforcement, here misnamed "positive feedback." (Positive feedback is properly, among other things, the howling of a public-address system turned up too high.) A quotation reproduced below speaks of "shaping" competencies in children, just as behaviorists speak of shaping behavior in rats.

Most disturbing is that LFM resembles operant conditioning in approach, as well as terminology. A behavioristic technology that flourished in the 1920s and 1930s, operant conditioning no longer has much currency among psychologists. In those days, it served primarily to teach rats and pigeons to press levers in order to receive food and water. There have been repeated efforts ever since to transplant the same techniques into the classroom, typically over objections from educators who believe there are fundamental differences between lever-pressing and reading, and between children and rats. CAI, too, was based primarily on operant techniques. Though each new attempt to introduce CAI was announced as the wave of the future and proclaimed its successes, each was gone within a few years.

Now, advocates of LFM have their own voluminous literature showing the method to be more effective than conventional classroom instruction. Occasionally, a little arrogance creeps in. In addition to past research, say Hyman and Cohen, "[W]e have

25 doctoral dissertations underway investigating LFM's instructional details. We no longer bother to ask how LFM compares to traditional curriculum; that is no longer an issue" (Hyman and Cohen 1979, p. 105). One of their doctoral candidates explains: "When you clearly define the required competencies, design instruction to shape those competencies, and monitor the process, and you compare such a technique to the traditional fuzzy, the results have got to be LFM! Why test the obvious?" Add the student's mentors, "Why, indeed!" (Hyman and Cohen 1979, p. 105).

In looking at such claims, it is important to know what the measures of student performance are. According to Block and Burns (1976, p. 13), the large majority of studies use "locally constructed measures." Presumably these tests are constructed for each experiment. But in comparing two teaching methods, it is not difficult to slant a test toward one or the other, sometimes inadvertently. LFM programs, for example, regularly use quizzes after each small instructional unit to ensure mastery. If items on the comparison test resemble these quizzes, the LFM student will have a considerable advantage, even where the test content applies equally to non-LFM students as well. It is also likely that two classrooms using different teaching methods will cover basically the same material with different emphases, opening another possibility for bias in the test results.

One major review article concludes the superiority of LFM by summarizing dozens of studies, yet offers little reassurance about test bias except for this remark: "As best we can determine, these examinations [used for comparison] contained no items *identical to* those that the mastery-taught students received during their diagnostic-progress testing" (Block and Burns 1976, p. 18, my emphasis). That is not enough, of course; if the format and the precise content of the questions are what LFM students are accustomed to, that alone is enough to bias the results in their favor. One of the coauthors, Robert B. Burns, agreed in a telephone conversation that bias of this kind remains a possibility.

It is safe to say, at a minimum, that LFM students consistently outperformed traditionally taught students on the particular tests used. Now, turn that around: Given a specific test, is it possible to design an LFM program around it that will be more effective than the corresponding conventional program? Yes, very probably—if the test examines fragmented knowledge and skills. LFM needs its content broken down cleanly into small steps, which becomes relatively easy if the test defining the content is fragmented itself. There are no studies, to my knowledge, directly on this point. Tending to bear it out, however, is a finding (tested among college students only) that LFM learning does not give as effective, consistent, or long-lasting results with "higher order behaviors" as it does with "lower order behaviors." Higher order behaviors here include "comprehension [!], application, analysis, synthesis, and evaluation skills," while lower order behaviors are those required to answer "knowledge items" on multiple-choice tests (Block and Burns 1976, p. 34). There is also some evidence that LFM may succeed in teaching even higher order skills, though the data on this issue are mixed.

In any event, LFM seems ideally suited to the kinds of learning needed for passing minimum competency exams. If this proves true in practice, LFM and methods like it will have great appeal wherever large numbers of students are failing the exams, i.e., in most of the minimum competency states. The LFM postulate that nearly all children are "equally capable of learning" (Glickman 1979, p. 100) is especially seductive. It is far from certain at this early stage, but the establishment of LFM-type instruction in minimum competency environments could result in wholesale changes in how we go about educating children. Schooling could be in for a major overhaul.

Whether such changes are for better or worse depends, once again, on one's view of the purpose of education. If the goal is to impart bits of skill and knowledge useful in passing certain kinds of tests, LFM may be the best thing to happen to schools in decades. If we expect something more from students—critical, creative thought, for example—then LFM might turn out to be a poor choice. The distinction may well become academic, however. In many school districts, the need to have students pass the tests will override all else. Whatever teaching method meets that single purpose will take precedence, regardless of its shortcomings in other respects.

LFM is only one of many possible side effects that minimum competency may spawn. Even without LFM, minimum competency will produce a variety of effects throughout education. Textbook publishers, always alert to their changing markets, will move in with materials keyed to the most common minimum competency objectives and to instructional techniques designed around those objectives. Test publishers (who in many cases put out the textbooks too) will reorient their instruments for all grades in order to alert teachers to those students who might later have trouble with the state tests. Changes in the tests will give the publishers' book divisions a further prod, because textbooks are judged in part on how well students using them perform on the tests. Colleges of education will feel growing pressure to train teachers-to-be in methods consistent with minimum competency—especially if states begin tying continued certification to student performance on the tests. In the face of limited resources, other school programs, such as those for handicapped children and for gifted and talented students, may find themselves in danger of losing funds. As we have noted before, minimum competency advocates may applaud such changes, seeing them as evidence that the schools are getting down to business at last.

In short, minimum competency will have substantial effects on education in terms of both method and content. The two tend to go hand in hand. Open education, we have seen, began with a method, which gave rise to new content. Minimum competency started by prescribing content, but it is certain to affect method as well; the new methods, in turn, will have further influence on content, and so on.

In the case of minimum competency, the method/content spiral runs the risk of winding down to a tight knot, a core of whatever "basics" the test-spawned instructional methods can handle most readily. That process can obscure the original goals of minimum competency, resulting in content that bears little relationship to what common sense tells us the basics really are. We may, in fact, find ourselves tied to a set of skills that may have been appropriate a generation ago, but have since become hopelessly unsuitable. The overriding importance of the tests will make curricular change all but impossible, except in those limited directions that improve test performance. Since test content will change slowly, if it changes at all, education will soon be frozen wherever the tests prevail. Minimum competency will act as a brake against most educational improvement.

This, too, may be part of the unspoken motivation underlying the minimum competency movement, i.e., to forestall future innovations such as those that produced open education, the new math, and *Man: A Course of Study*. And a stasis in education would not necessarily be bad, if it froze good educational practice and if educational needs remained the same. As to quality of educational practice, however, the tests are likely to hinder it on the whole, for reasons set out in the last chapter. Nor do educational needs remain the same. In elementary mathematics particularly, recent changes in the technological environment call for new emphases in schooling. In math, the freezing effect of minimum competency will bar badly needed reforms that are already overdue.

Indeed, the case of mathematics is an excellent example of how minimum competency's uncritical reverence for the "basics" of the past can do education real harm. The situation is ironic: Changing needs in mathematics directly address the "real-life tasks" that are the rationale for minimum competency, yet minimum competency frustrates any chance of meeting those needs. Moreover, even if society's mathematical needs had remained the same, prompt educational reform would still be necessary. Schooling in mathematics has been a consistent failure for many generations. By inhibiting meaningful improvement, minimum competency now ensures that the same failures will continue indefinitely into the future.

Mathematics thus provides an especially clear instance of how minimum competency impairs curriculum. The consequences may be no more severe than those for reading and other areas, but they are more evident and easier to foresee. For that reason and by way of example, I shall devote the rest of this chapter to a discussion of where mathematics education has been, where it must go next, and why minimum competency threatens to keep it from getting there for a long time.

It is important to note at the outset that the schools never successfully taught mathematics to more than a small fraction of students. When Jerrold Zacharias and I first said this publicly in the early 1970s (Lazarus 1974*b* and Zacharias 1974), we raised some hostile eyebrows. But since then, there has grown up a substantial industry devoted to alleviating "math anxiety" among adults (Tobias 1980) and its corollary, mathematical incompetence. Even the federal government has joined the act with programs aimed at attracting women and minorities to mathematics and related fields.

The widespread concern with mathematical troubles has encouraged recognition that the schools are doing a poor job of teaching math in the first place. Skeptical readers should stop the next ten people they meet (not teachers or academics, please) and ask two questions: (1) "How do you feel about mathematics?" and (2) "What mathematics have you done in the past month?" It is a rare sample of ten that yields more than one or two positive answers to either question. No one, however, has yet troubled to verify such informal findings with a proper survey.

The math anxiety movement originally had two sources. One grew out of feminist concerns, with the realization that far fewer women than men are mathematically prepared on entering college (Sells 1978). The result is a kind of self-imposed sexual discrimination in education, and later in employment. It is significant that the first popular article on math anxiety appeared in *Ms* magazine (Tobias 1975). Much of the early work on alleviating math anxiety, launched by campus feminists, concentrated on undoing the social and educational pressures that turn girls away from mathematics early in school.

The other source of the math anxiety movement arose among educators who wondered why most adults cannot or will not perform the mathematics they supposedly learned in school. Most people, it seems, are willing to go far out of their way to avoid mathematics. Calling this condition "mathophobia," Zacharias located its source chiefly in elementary school. He blames the elementary curriculum in particular: Tedious, painstaking, unforgiving, conceptually difficult, it offers the child no useful payoff (Lazarus 1975). Many children become bogged down after the first few grades. Nearly all opt out by high school, typically as soon as curriculum requirements allow it. The experience for most children is overwhelmingly negative. In consequence, only a small fraction of adults of either sex are comfortable with mathematics, though the percentage is doubtless even smaller for women than for men.

From either the feminist or the curriculum perspective, mathematics education has been unsuccessful. Though most children take at least eight years of mathematics in school, at a cost to taxpayers of billions of dollars annually, hardly any adults seem to have benefited from those years of study. More college freshmen feel they need remedial help in mathematics than in any other subject area (Dearman and Plisko 1979). A miniscule percentage of students go on to specialize in mathematics, the sciences, or engineering; another handful choose areas that require less demanding forms of mathematics. But the great majority of students give up the whole business with a sigh of relief and wonder for the rest of their lives what that relief might have cost them in lost opportunities.

It is hard to imagine now, but the national math problem went unrecognized until the mid-1970s. The new math, which came about fifteen years earlier, addressed wholly different concerns. In an era of Sputnik and the cold war, the new math aimed to improve the United States's international standing in science and technology. Educational reform in other subject areas was then showing great success. Enthusiasm ran high in those days of the early 1960s; Sputnik had made available great sums of money, and anything seemed possible. It was an ideal *zeitgeist* in which to launch a massive overhaul.

The thinking of the times, moreover, dictated that reform question everything thus far taken for granted in the field. The more entrenched a belief, the more suspect it became. The new math developers adopted that philosophy, with reasoning that went very roughly like this:

1. Children study mostly arithmetic;

2. They find arithmetic hard because, as taught, it consists of arbitrary rules;

3. The remedy is to teach the mathematical principles behind the rules first, so that the rules will make sense.

The mathematical principles that make arithmetic rules work are pretty abstract stuff, usually taught in advanced undergraduate courses. (Actually, it's the arithmetic that makes the abstract principles work, though the mathematicians involved chose to look at it the other way around.) The required sophistication did not seem like much of an obstacle. A belief prevailed at the time that children of any age could learn just about anything, if properly taught. In effect, the new math developers rewrote advanced material for the primary grades and adapted everything else to it. The developers made a point of stressing that arithmetic remained the fundamental goal.

Like many other reforms, the new math looked good on paper. In practice, though, the mathematical principles as taught made no more sense to children than the arbitrary rules of arithmetic and for many were harder to learn. In the old days, for example, if someone asked a second grader why 3 times 4 is the same as 4 times 3, the answer was a shrugged, "It just is, that's all." With a new-math second grader, the conversation ran a little longer:

"Because multiplication is commutative."

"Why is that?"

"It's an axiom."

"What makes it an axiom?"

"It just is, that's all."

Same result by a different route. Parents were dismayed; they did not understand what their children were talking about and could not help. It comes as a shock to learn from one's eight-year-old offspring that 2 + 2 = 10, a correct result in "base 4" arithmetic. Many teachers had insufficient training; they could not help much either, except to parrot the teacher's manual.

And despite some early studies showing that new-math students learned better, a consensus later emerged that the axioms, change of number base, set theory, and the other special topics were of little real value in teaching arithmetic.

The first publisher to notice a shift in the wind issued a text series using a "basal skills" approach—that means rote arithmetic—which quickly swept the market. Other publishers joined in; school systems dropped new math in droves; and in an amazingly short time, old-fashioned arithmetic prevailed once again. The nation was back to basics.

Parenthetically, though, some elements of the new math did prove exceedingly useful, especially the work of David Page and Bob Davis. Both men have remarkable insight into children's mathematical thinking and translated their findings into effective instruction. Neither, I suspect, would have identified himself with the new math as that term is generally construed; Davis even took the trouble to write an article pointing out that "new math" lumped several very different trends under one name (Davis 1974). But their work was new; it was mathematical; and it coincided with the new math chronologically. This was enough to condemn it in the eyes of the counterreform, and their contributions of that time are now largely lost to educational practice. No doubt the same is true of other valuable work in math education developed during the same period.

Once the decision was made to abandon new math, there was nowhere else to turn but to old math. Even if other alternatives had been available, the mood was strongly "back to basics." Educators, having just weathered one unsuccessful attempt at reform, were unlikely to attempt another while the wounds were still fresh. The old ways seemed safest, and their readoption inevitable.

Old math also had an appealing social logic. Arithmetic is, most of all, the mathematics of buying and selling. Even the minimum competency word problems in arithmetic are mostly about money. And as every consumer partakes of the nation's commercial life, everybody needs to know arithmetic—or so the reasoning goes. There may also have been a historical logic as well. As it happens, the schools teach elementary arithmetic in just about the same sequence that mankind invented it over the millennia, save only that we spare children the perversions of computing in Babylonian and Roman numerals. (Even the Romans computed mostly with movable counters, not with Xs and Vs.) In accordance with the principle that ontogeny recapitulates phylogeny,[3] it is tempting to think that this same sequence is somehow the most "natural" one in which to impress arithmetic on a growing mind.

The return to old math presented two problems, however. The old ways had never worked well; few adult alumni of old-math elementary schools can perform arithmetic fluently, and most are burdened with an intense dislike for mathematics. And just when the new math declined and fell, there occurred a technological revolution that left most of elementary school mathematics utterly useless. Calculators became cheap. People bought them by the millions. Before that, most people had avoided doing arithmetic altogether, but by 1976 it took only six or seven dollars to make anyone an expert. As the 1980s opened, households without at least one calculator were rare. The vast majority of adults had stopped even trying to do arithmetic by hand.

The schools' response to these developments was a little bizarre, though understandable in light of their recent experience with the new math. The schools simply pretended calculators did not exist and went right along with the now pointless task of teaching long division. The children, who know a head in the sand when they see it, protested. Finding no support for their good sense, they saved up their lunch money for calculators and used them surreptitiously.

The schools' position was not unlike illuminating the classroom with candles after there were electric lights everywhere else. Today, in fact, the elementary classroom is just about the only place in the country where anyone does arithmetic with pencil and paper. Nobody has to do longhand arithmetic on the job anymore, or at home either. Long division is considered an essential skill for people under twelve, but for no one else.

The schools had to justify this stand, of course, and they did it on essentially moral grounds. The calculator is a crutch, they said, and right-thinking people do not depend on crutches.

(Students of history will recall similar moral arguments against the use of anesthesia, airplanes, canned foods, and just about every other innovation that makes people's lives easier.) There were practical arguments. What if the student is caught someday without a calculator? What if the battery runs down? Calculator advocates patiently replied that since few adults can do much arithmetic anyway without a calculator, a run-down battery is no serious deficit. But the schools insisted that battery failure justifies taking up an hour a day of every child's life for six or seven years, doing work proved to turn most children away from mathematics altogether. Even the appearance of the liquid-crystal calculator, whose batteries last for years, failed to shake this reasoning.

Research began. Most of the early studies were devoted to proving that students with calculators learn longhand arithmetic just as well as students without. Though it attracted considerable interest, this question is rather beside the point because calculators largely replace the need for arithmetic skills in the first place. Using calculators to teach these skills amounts to using horse-drawn wagons to deliver Mack trucks.

At the same time, other people were thinking about more productive uses for calculators in mathematics education. That work began well before the present controversy arose. Back in 1972 and 1973, when the machines still cost over a hundred dollars, people familiar with the electronics industry were confidently predicting the drastic price reductions that later, in fact, came about. Most educators scoffed then, but a few foresaw the impact that calculators would have on daily life and so expected (wrongly, as it turned out) that curriculum would change accordingly. Thus, they considered what topics could safely be dropped, what new ones must be added, and how the sequencing of material could change once freed from the constraints imposed by the structure of arithmetic. The result was a fascinating glimpse of elementary mathematics that many children could enjoy and that would stand them in good stead later in life.

Problem solving received major attention in all such plans. (For example, see Lazarus 1978.) Though always advertised as a major component of the elementary curriculum, problem solving has had little emphasis in practice, especially in the primary grades. There is good reason: Until fifth or sixth grade, students' arithmetical repertoires are too limited to be useful. Stilted word problems, in fact, are just about all young children can handle: "If Janie has 9 candies and gives 4 to Kevin . . . " That sort of problem is easily tailored to students' abilities in each grade, but the results are necessarily boring, pointless, and contrived.

With calculators, on the other hand, even very young children can tackle problems far more elaborate and truer to life. Most important, calculators free students to concentrate on thinking through the problem, rather than on the mechanics of the arithmetic involved. Since calculators make all numbers almost equally easy to handle, problem situations can come from topics that interest children. How many seconds have you been alive? How many more games must the local team win to place first in the league? When a singer sells a million records, how high a stack would that make? A fast-food chain claims to have sold so many billion hamburgers; is that reasonably possible? In other kinds of problems, children can even use data they gather themselves.

Calculators also promise to reduce math anxiety at its source, the elementary classroom. Arithmetic, particularly in its more complicated forms, causes much of the trouble now. Calculators would eliminate the worst of that (though some simple arithmetic will always remain essential), and using calculators is something most children enjoy. Even if no greater number of students developed a positive love of mathematics, probably far fewer than today would come to hate it.

A calculator-based curriculum would still require a certain amount of arithmetic, including the multiplication table and other operations on small numbers. It would also need new material not currently taught in any depth: problem-solving techniques, approximation, estimation, precision and error, and other topics important to using mathematics in realistic situations. As long as the problems themselves are interesting, which becomes relatively easy with calculators, there should be little difficulty in making these new ideas both accessible and attractive. And since elaborate arithmetic plays practically no part in more advanced mathematics,[4] the curriculum would provide adequate preparation for the small proportion of students who go on to become mathematicians or scientists.

In short, a much improved curriculum in elementary mathematics has been practical for a few years now. The ideas outlined here found little support when first promulgated in the early and mid-1970s (Lazarus 1974*a* and 1975). But in the years since, educators have gradually been building a consensus along the same lines. Scholars generally agree now that calculators can no longer be ignored and that problem solving must become an important curricular focus.

Support remains softer among teachers and their supervisors but is growing in that sector too. Groups and associations concerned with math education are taking public stands that favor deemphasis of rote arithmetic in favor of problem solving. The first to express support was the National Council of Supervisors of Mathematics (1976). And while this book was still in the typewriter, the National Council of Teachers of Mathematics (NCTM) issued an "Agenda for Action: Recommendations for School Mathematics of the 1980s." The council recommended among other things that

1. problem solving be the focus of school mathematics in the 1980s;

2. basic skills in mathematics be defined to encompass more than computational facility;

3. mathematics programs take full advantage of the power of calculators and computers at all grade levels;

4. the success of mathematics programs and student learning be evaluated by a wider range of measures than conventional testing (National Council of Teachers of Mathematics 1980).

In the accompanying press release, NCTM speaks in even stronger terms, making problem-solving ability "*the* top priority" (their emphasis), and describing as "unproductive" a lot of computation with large numbers. Other experts speak of increasing students' intuitive fluency with numbers, a goal that accords well with early introduction of calculators (Suydam 1976). Even publishers—usually the most conservative element—are interested; one major schoolbook company recently offered an unprecedented advance against royalties to a private group to develop a curriculum using calculators, though the group had to decline when additional support for the work proved unavailable.

The situation in math education has thus become a paradox. There is a problem, centuries old: Children don't learn to do mathematics in school; they learn to despise it. With calculators, technology has outdated part of that problem and offers a way to help solve the rest of it. The people best informed about math education concur on the route to take. Commercial interest is evident. Yet progress has been stopped. Worse, it will probably remain stopped for many years.

Part of the reason, as I have suggested, is an unhappy memory of the new math and the consequent reluctance to risk another failure. The connection between new math and these plans is mostly emotional, however. With its emphasis on practicality and real-world orientation, the curriculum sketched here takes a direction precisely opposite to the abstractions of the new math. Besides, memory of the new math is gradually fading and should not remain a significant obstacle to improvement for much longer. The mention of "realistic problems" and the thought of children collecting their own data also remind some people of open education. Perhaps the ideas draw opposition from that emotional association as well.

A more important barrier is, or soon will be, the minimum competency tests. Indeed, their role here exemplifies the potential that minimum competency has to inhibit useful learning. The tests, we have seen, focus on the basics of generations past: arithmetic and its most contrived, simplistic "applications." There is no room on the tests for creative problem solving or fluency with mathematical ideas. Consequently, these things have no place in a curriculum whose main priority is preparation for the tests.

There is a second paradox in math education, a more serious one. Ostensibly, the tests ensure that students are prepared for the world outside the classroom. Yet the mathematical needs in that world have changed. There may have been some justification for giving the present tests to students who graduated in 1970, but there is no rational basis for requiring them of students who leave school in 1980 and after. We are insisting on minimum competence in useless skills.

In the case of mathematics, the tests themselves frustrate the very purposes for which they were established. Educators are now in a position to give students much better preparation for adult life than they currently receive—yet are prevented from doing so, in part, by the very tests meant to guarantee that preparation.

Major curriculum change takes a long time, typically at least five years of research, pilot studies, development, and evaluation. It is correspondingly expensive. The mathematics curriculum outlined here would cost at least a few million dollars to develop and try out, though that is a small fraction of the sums wasted every year in trying to teach current mathematics. But as long as the product's adoption is virtually barred by minimum competency tests that call for old skills, no one can invest the money and personal effort that the task would require. Moreover, even if there were interest in revising the minimum competency tests to suit a sensible curriculum, the new tests could not be used until the curriculum was in place and operating. Each must precede the other. The outcome: stalemate.

Other subject areas are just as susceptible to the stalemate, although it is especially apparent in mathematics. Improvement in all of the minimum competency subject areas will be impeded in just the same way. In writing, for example, there is growing interest in stressing expository techniques as a way to promote students' fluency on paper. But unless the approach delivers good scores on the tests, it is unlikely to take hold, regardless of its merits. In subject areas that are not tested, the situation is even worse, for those areas are in danger of being deemphasized to the point of neglect—science, for example, and foreign languages. The interest and the money necessary for meaningful improvement in these subjects will be hard to find.

The outlook is discouraging all around. The tests are likely to trivialize curriculum as a whole because of the political need to ensure that some minimum number of students are certified "competent." And the mathematics example shows how the tests' very existence can lock useless education into place. All this, from a program intended to raise the quality of American education! There is something very wrong with a mechanism that interferes with its own goals.

Notes

1. The rough symmetry between achievement tests and curriculum means that neither one can change without a corresponding change in the other. This fact has greatly impeded curriculum reform, for test revision is so expensive as to make test publishers very cautious. Curriculum improvement must show exceptional promise before the tests will change to accommodate it, and the schools typically cannot adopt the new program until the new tests are available. Thus, big changes are easier than small ones. The first of the major reforms in the last generation, PSSC Physics, prompted changes in the SAT to reflect its new content. Similarly, the new math led to revision of elementary achievement tests. I can think of no other comparable examples but do know of several excellent curricular programs that died on the vine, partly because they were inconsistent with the tests in use. (PSSC Physics was developed by the Physical Science Study Committee, based at MIT, and involved scientists and educators nationwide.)

2. Zacharias's best known work in physics is his invention of the cesium-beam clock, sometimes called the "atomic clock," which now provides all standards of time for the world. He also made important contributions to defense technology, including work on the atomic bomb program during World War II, antisubmarine warfare in the 1950s, and devices that made the DEW line practical. For 12 years he served on the president's Science Advisory Committee. In 1956, at the request of James R. Killian, then president of the Massachusetts Institute of Technology, Zacharias agreed to spend three months on educational problems. He is still at it. His PSSC Physics was the first of the major curriculum reforms and inspired many of the improvements that emerged over the following two decades. Zacharias had an active hand in many of the other improvements as well; he most recently helped to launch the current movement to reform testing practices. After founding the nonprofit Education Development Center in 1958 to distribute PSSC materials, Zacharias was instrumental in building the company into a global leader in educational improvement, with operations and programs all over the world. One informal indication of his influence is that officers of the National Science Foundation still measure large grants in "Zachs," with one Zach equal to approximately a quarter-million dollars. For the past year or two, Zacharias's main interest has been the task of providing the American public with accurate and understandable information about the nation's energy needs, resources, and options.

3. For readers who cut that particular class in elementary biology, the principle is that the growing fetus of any species reproduces over a few weeks the same forms as its ancestors did during the entire course of evolution. The human fetus, for example, goes through a fish stage, a reptile stage, and so on. While the principle is true in a very general way, it does not stand up to detailed examination. My analogy, which may not withstand much examination either, is that school leads each child through the development of arithmetic by way of the same sequence of stages in which arithmetic "evolved" over human history.

4. Fractions are a notorious trouble spot in elementary mathematics, particularly computation with lowest common denominators. The combination of calculators and metric measurement will eventually render calculation on all except the simplest fractions unnecessary. Yet some teachers want to keep teaching lowest common denominator in the intermediate grades, solely on the grounds that students who take algebra several years later will find it useful. The students will, if they remember it; but it seems more sensible to shift the topic to the algebra course. This is the only example that comes to mind of complicated arithmetic that serves a purpose in more advanced work.

5

Competency Testing of Minority and Handicapped Students

M inimum competency tests have to be absolutely fair. Otherwise even the staunchest advocate must have second thoughts; no one can endorse a test that fails students who have the skills to pass. Errors the other way—passing students who should fail—do less harm to individuals, but collectively still threaten the goal of a meaningful diploma.

It seems that most commentators have taken for granted that the tests are basically fair, though attorney Merle McClung (1977, 1978) persistently raises the question of fairness. More often, criticism is on other grounds, most of which we have already examined. Perhaps this is because the tests look fair, at least superficially. And many of the people whose training and experience might alert them to the problems—the professionals in psychometrics—have an interest in seeing the movement go forward. There is a lot of money to be made in minimum competency testing, to be blunt about it, and a lot of opportunities for professional advancement. There is also a natural tendency for professionals to support the profession to which they have devoted their working lives.

When nonprofessionals examine tests, even tests for young children, most have a tendency to "take the test" themselves as a kind of game. It is fascinating to watch a roomful of well-educated adults going over a third-grade test, careful not to look at the correct answers until they have figured them out for themselves. Harmless, perhaps, but the game can distort the review process. Most lay people will approve the test as long as the scoring key agrees with their own answers and challenge only the items that they themselves get wrong. The subtleties likely to distract a third grader—or a twelfth grader, for that matter—often go unnoticed in the flush of success.

Moreover, educators and lay people alike have great respect for the supposed objectivity and impartiality of multiple-choice instruments. The respect comes in part from the tables of statistics that test publishers provide on item analysis, reliability, and validation studies. The columns of numbers look impressive. We saw in Chapter 2 that studies and statistics give little protection against a poor test. Pointing to the numbers, nevertheless, the psychometric community has insisted over the years that such tests have been proven to measure what they are supposed to and that they treat all students alike. As a result, the overall feeling in the educational community and among legislators is that the tests are good. Not perfect, of course—no one claims that—but good enough, and certainly better than nothing.

"Not perfect" turns out to be a serious problem, however, in the case of minimum competency. In principle, no test can distinguish among students with absolute precision; in practice, the level of precision falls well below the absolute. A limited degree of test error is acceptable in some circumstances, where decisions based on the errors can be easily corrected. But where the effects of a low score are important and permanent, there can be little tolerance for error. A student denied a high school diploma because he scores too low on a minimum competency test will have every reason to object if his score might have been invalid. He will take little comfort in the school's claim that the test is, after all, accurate for 95 percent of his classmates. The student may also have a good case in court.

Test error, in short, opens the possibility for a new kind of social wrong—one potentially more serious than the much-publicized problems with the SAT and the admission tests for professional schools. The more drastic the sanction, the better the test must be. When the sanction is all but irreparable, as with diploma denial, the test has to be just about perfect. The technology of testing, unfortunately, is not yet that advanced.

The social wrong does not stop with test error. Let us imagine, for the sake of discussion, a scenario in which an absolutely perfect test of minimum competency is available. Its reliability and validity are unimpeachable. Any two students with equivalent skills will always get exactly the same score. The test offers a meaningful cutoff point, below which the student's lack of functional literacy can justify withholding his diploma. The test (this is fantasy, remember) is exactly fair in every respect.

Even with a perfect test, however, important problems remain. A motto by Paul F-Brandwein makes this point; it ought to hang in every testing office in the country:

THERE IS NOTHING SO UNEQUAL
AS THE EQUAL TREATMENT OF UNEQUALS[1]

Whatever else it may be, the American student body is unequal. Its diversity is staggering, among both the students and the expectations that society has for them.

In the old days, which ended roughly with the Supreme Court's call for school desegregation in 1954, students came in two main categories: smart and stupid. The smart ones stayed in school; the stupid ones dropped out to find work that required little education. Except among a few progressive educators, there was little concern with why some students did better in school than others. Instead, a few simplistic assumptions went largely unchallenged: Smart parents had smart children; white people had smarter children than black people; and third generation Americans had smarter children than immigrants, at least for the first generation or two. The schools took children pretty much as they came and simply allowed the ones who couldn't make it to fail. Why they couldn't make it, and what became of them after they left school—these were the students' problems, or their parents'. The schools concentrated on those students who, in the phrase of the time, had "the capacity to benefit from an education."

We need not trace in detail the profound changes in attitude that came with the late 1950s and the 1960s, except to note two of the forces. First, the need for unskilled labor dried up due to mechanization and automation. Second, the Supreme Court insisted on equal educational opportunity for all children, regardless of race. Later the Congress added: and regardless of handicap.

The schools had been accustomed to ignoring student diversity. Teaching was primarily directed to the white middle class, and students whom that instruction did not suit were left to drop by the wayside. But that was not "equal educational opportunity" and so it had to change. The schools gradually took on the responsibility of teaching the students they had previously overlooked.

With that, and with the liberal attitudes that swept the country in the 1960s, came an important shift in emphasis: When a student failed to learn, it was the school's fault. Regardless of race, language, or home environment, the schools were expected, and expected themselves, to teach everyone. It was no longer acceptable to "blame the victim" — a popular phrase in those days. There were no more stupid children (except perhaps for the certifiably retarded); children who could not make it in school became known instead as "educationally disadvantaged." The change in terminology reflected a shift in responsibility, because it was now the school's task to provide educational advantages. A failing child became squarely the school's problem.

It is hard to overemphasize the importance of this change. It departed from the educational experience of every nation throughout history. Universal literacy had long been a goal in the industrialized part of the world, but never before had a nation seriously undertaken to include in that goal each and every child, regardless of social background. (There is one possible exception. For hundreds of years, the Jewish people have insisted on literacy for all males, though not for females until comparatively recent times. Boys attain manhood at the age of thirteen in the Bar Mitzvah ceremony. Reduced to its secular essentials, the ceremony is a public demonstration of the boy's ability to read aloud in Hebrew. And as the rights and obligations of adulthood are withheld from the boy until he completes the ceremony successfully, the Bar Mitzvah amounts to something very much like a minimum competency test. There are, of course, religious implications to the ceremony that overshadow the competency aspects.)

The belief that every child could be educated to a high standard coincided with a period of national self-confidence in other areas. This was the time of the New Frontier, the Great Society, and a man on the moon by the end of the decade. Vietnam was still a minor skirmish. A rapidly expanding economy, not yet beset by warfare and OPEC, made huge amounts of federal money available. Psychology and sociology took rapid strides, providing a phalanx of trained experts ready to take that money in exchange for promises to solve the nation's social problems.

The same period also saw the promotion of liberal ideas on human nature, particularly in racial matters. The centuries-old belief in black people's inferiority finally met its end, at least among most of the educated. Legislation, long overdue, ensured that even people who still maintained the old prejudices could not exercise them in such basic areas of life as housing, employment, and credit. There grew up, in place of the old racist view, the counterproposition that all people are essentially alike, save for superficial differences in appearance.

Thoughtful black leaders saw a problem lurking in the liberalism, however. In a white-dominated society, the view that all people are alike is liable to take on a particular slant — that all people are like white people. The disavowal of racism could lead to something almost as bad, the submersion of black culture. To many blacks, the price of equality looked like an exchange of rich African heritage for middle-class culture, which, even in the eyes of its members, left much to be desired. It seems unfair that a people would have to give up its values, its dialect, and everything else that makes it unique in order to gain what it should have had all along — simply the same rights and privileges as everyone else.

It is thus no coincidence that the "black is beautiful" movement gained strength just when white liberal society was reaching out to help blacks, often with the best intentions, but with little thought to the consequences for black culture. Offered a choice between subjection and submersion, many blacks insisted that a third option was possible, that of cultural coexistence. And no group can survive intact within a larger group without a strong sense of pride.

Educators, for the most part, understood well enough the importance of black pride, at least as long as its expression did not disturb school routine. Most educators saw the need to respect black culture and values, particularly music, literature, and art, and to make these available in the classroom for both white and black children. A few schools went so far as to celebrate Kwanza with Christmas and Hanukkah and to incorporate works by contemporary black authors into the required curriculum, along with carefully selected episodes from black history. The contributions of blacks to American history received considerable emphasis, with Benjamin Banneker singled out (for some reason) as a special folk hero in the early grades.

At the same time, though, the schools were responsible for educating black children in what amounts to the white image—standard English, the history of Western Europe, and the thought processes and values that came to the United States with its white founders and immigrants. There was little room, in practice, for more than passing reference to black heritage.

Even so, the majority of black parents favored integration. The segregated schools in black neighborhoods were terrible, by and large, and had not done much themselves to nourish black values. With integration, at least the quality of education would improve, and black children would have a better chance of successfully competing with educated whites. The possibility of escaping from the vicious cycle of poverty, for many, made even the dilution of culture a price worth paying.

Immediately following the Supreme Court order to desegregate, the equation seemed simple enough: All people are alike, and therefore, equal educational opportunity should lead to equal attainment. By the early 1960s, however, it was clear that the equation was not holding up as expected. All people were alike—except that black children as a group did not perform in school as well as their white classmates, even where desegregation was complete. The anomaly demanded an explanation, one that did not revive ideas of racial inferiority. (A racist attempt at explanation came a little later, with the work of Jensen [1969].) Only one explanation could resolve the dilemma within the prevailing social ideology: namely, that black children had an unfair disadvantage due to poverty and discrimination, that is, due to the past prejudice of whites. After all, poor white children had trouble in school too, and so did children from other minority groups that were targets of discrimination.

Psychologists rushed in with armloads of data on early learning, early malnutrition, and urban overcrowding. One study even pointed to the effects of environmental deprivation on the weights of rats' brains, though its authors considerately refrained from gathering human data. Taken together, the research offered an explanation that saved face all around, except perhaps in the homes of poor blacks. By the time a black child started school at age five or six, said the investigators, it was too late. The disadvantage was already insurmountable.

The cry went up for "early intervention," and the money flowed. Head Start rolled across the nation. When it became apparent that many Head Start children slowed down after leaving the program, there was Follow Through to help them. Joan Ganz Cooney put together $8 million for the first year of "Sesame Street" and soon had America's toddlers chanting the alphabet from 4:00 to 4:58 P.M. daily. "The Electric Company" came soon after. Noting the success of these two shows, the federal government gave each its own line item in the budget and stepped in with millions more each year for additional television programming aimed at minority children.[2] Uncountable sums of other funding, in addition to the massive Title I expenditures,[3] tried to compensate in other ways for the effects of poverty and past discrimination.

In retrospect, there is still not much agreement on whether these intervention programs were successful. People's judgments seem to depend as much on their original expectations as on the actual outcomes. Those looking for dramatic improvement in educational results—i.e., test scores—have on the whole been disappointed. For example, the National Assessment of Educational Progress consistently shows that the performance of black children, though improving in some areas, remains substantially below that of whites. On the other hand, I know of no study that tracks the long-term academic progress of students exposed to particular programs. For some of the students now turning up in the National Assessment data, Head Start and the other programs may simply have come too late.

The experience with minimum competency testing so far is similarly disturbing: The rate of failure among blacks is high, much higher than among whites.[4] Here, too, educational improvements that currently might be helping young children may have come too late for today's test takers. That was the court's conclusion in one lawsuit we shall examine in a later chapter.

Still, it is no comfort to a black family to be told: Wait—maybe your younger children will do better. Some people would rather believe that the poor performance of blacks is intended by the white authorities in order "to exclude blacks, poor whites, Indians . . . from the educational process, and later on from the job market" (Zakariya 1979). The person quoted here was suing the North Carolina Competency Test Commission in a class action on behalf of minority students in that state.

More moderate black parents can correctly point out that competency testing tends to be an aftereffect of desegregation. It may be historical accident. But if not, then the minimum competency goal of "protecting standards" takes on a neoracist quality, as if the standards need protection mainly from blacks. Indeed, as Merle McClung (1978) observes, competency testing can lead to resegregation within the schools, rather than among them, in schools that track students according to test results. Resegregation in society at large is also not difficult to foresee, if competency testing results in a class of unemployables who are disproportionately minority people.

The argument is sometimes made that minimum competency testing is actually helpful to young minority people: As long as a high school diploma gives no assurance of needed skills, an employer must determine for himself whether a candidate has the education needed for the job. Employers who are prejudiced, the argument goes, are more likely to see black candidates as unqualified. Once the diploma reflects a certain standard, then a black applicant who has a diploma will be harder to discriminate against. The argument must be weighed, however, in terms of two other considerations: first, whether a "meaningful diploma" would in fact cut down appreciably on discrimination in hiring—a doubtful proposition at best—and second, the discrimination involved in qualifying for the diploma in the first place. In balance, the minimum competency program seems to promise blacks far more harm than good.

Black students are now asking the courts to intervene on their behalf. The resulting decisions will complicate the legal maze in which schools are operating already and sound legal decisions are impossible without a good understanding of the facts. More important, educators must, for their own consciences, confront the possibility of unfair discrimination in the competency tests. It would be reprehensible to hold black and white students to what are ostensibly the same standards if in fact there are greater obstacles in the paths of blacks. That situation would offend our most fundamental ideas of fair play.

When it comes to specifics, there are really only a few possible explanations for blacks' relatively poor showing on the competency tests:

1. Racism: black children are not as smart as white children;

2. Early environment: black children develop more slowly in intellect due to early deprivation;

3. Later environment: black parents and peers do not give school the same priority that white parents and peers do;

4. Test bias: something in the tests themselves makes them unfair to black children;

5. Unequal schooling: black children's education does not equip them for the tests as well as white children's.

We can dismiss the first possibility outright, that of differential intelligence. No doubt some school administrators hold this view privately, but few knowledgeable psychologists nowadays take it seriously.

The other four possibilities hold the school responsible in varying degrees for the student's failure. The last two—test bias and unequal education—are especially egregious. If either is fact, the minimum competency program is simply unfair. A student would then have his diploma withheld for reasons totally outside his control—but under the control of the same people who withhold the diploma from him.

Yet the environmental possibilities are not really within the student's control either. Let us suppose, for the sake of argument, that explanation (2) or (3) above is correct. Early deprivation or later environment, let us say, can account for the high failure rate among blacks—though no one could actually make this claim on the evidence available. If, however, the student's home and neighborhood environment were known to be responsible, the schools could answer two ways. They might say, "Tough luck. We run a school here, not a social agency. If the kids don't want an education, that's their problem." Or, the schools could respond, "It's our fault. We're obviously doing something wrong. It's our job to educate black kids along with white kids, and we're just not meeting their needs."

Either way, however, whether the schools accept the responsibility or not, they are still discriminating against black students. Simply giving a test on which black children perform poorly is an act of discrimination, made significant by the consequences of failure. The tough-luck schools would claim they are discriminating on the basis of ability, not race. More sympathetic schools would acknowledge that racial factors can affect the results and would strengthen their efforts to compensate.

To the courts, the question of educators' *intent* to discriminate is central. If intent is there, educators are likely to be held liable, perhaps even if the school is trying to do better. The Supreme Court has struggled for years to define intent to discriminate and to tell the lower courts what evidence to look for. In the next chapter, I shall apply some of the decisions from the past few years to the minimum competency situation. It appears that school systems will be hard pressed to escape an imputation of intent if they can be proven to have discriminated in the education prior to the test.

Beyond intent is a more practical and urgent question. Given that black students are doing poorly on the tests, who must correct this? Is it the schools' job, or can the schools sit back and wait for student motivation and early development to improve?

Again, we are only assuming for now that these are the real problems.

For at least three reasons, the schools can expect to bear the burden of correcting racial differences. First, the responsibility follows from the trend discussed earlier, that of seeking to educate students who in decades past would have been allowed, perhaps encouraged, to drop out. Second, the schools are bound by law to provide equal educational opportunity for all students. And third, the promise of equal opportunity is what makes minimum competency testing even superficially acceptable. Without it, the program would be hopelessly unfair.

How equal must the opportunities be to justify competency testing? Uniform opportunities are not enough; recall Brandwein's comment about the equal treatment of unequals. Equal opportunities must instead be different, for different students. There is some violence to synonyms here, but the concept seems right; we have long accepted that equal opportunity can require compensatory and remedial education. So the question becomes, paradoxically, how different is equal enough?

If we could somehow educate individually, meeting each student's individual needs, there could be little objection to competency testing on equal opportunity grounds. Every student would have, in a sense, an equal chance at success. That kind of schooling is impossible, except for the very wealthy. But to the extent that we fall short of it, the competency test becomes an unequal burden. The schools as a fact serve some students worse than others. Despite some improvements, the schools are falling short most conspicuously with minority children.

In practice, as a result, the testing program shifts responsibility for failure back upon the student, whether or not he can rightly be held to blame. It is not the school system that suffers when a diploma is withheld, but the student who must go through life a certified illiterate. The failing student is punished for a failure that is largely outside his power to prevent. He must pay, in short, for the school's failure to keep its impossible promises.

In that light, the reasons for black students' high rate of

failure on the minimum competency tests may not be so important, for all the reasons erode the testing program's claim of fairness. Whether the problem is test bias, unsuitable schooling, or preschool and out-of-school environments, there is not much the student can do about it. Often the schools cannot either, especially if the problems begin at home. But in that event, the schools are hardly entitled to penalize further the same people they are unable to help. Life in this country is hard enough for a minority child, and all the more so for one whose education has been weak.

Instead of a diploma, perhaps students who fail the tests should be issued an official apology from the state department of education. And perhaps states unwilling to provide apologies ought not to set up competency tests either, unless they can prove that their educational opportunities are really equal for everyone.

I mention in passing the possibility that the tests themselves are biased against black students. That is ultimately a question for the courts, and Chapter 7 mentions the factors that one court considered. The question is a hard one because it rests on individual perceptions of particular test questions.

For certain nonracial minorities, however, the issue of test bias is much clearer. The two groups most likely to raise a challenge are those whose native language is not English and those who are handicapped. Almost all the problems noted in this chapter apply to these groups as well as to racial minorities, but these two populations also have special problems of their own.

Through most of American history, one goal of the schools has been to teach English to the children of immigrants. The reasoning was once persuasive. As English was the only American language, some degree of facility with it was essential to survival in this country. Even today, the naturalization laws require a test of English, except for old people.

The instructional method was simple enough, though brutal. All classes were conducted in English only, whether or not students understood what was going on. Older children, newly arrived, either sat towering over the first graders, humiliated, or else among their age-mates, hopelessly confused. The first generation often dropped out of school early, a sacrifice to the system, and the second generation assimilated. Many groups resented this systematic assault on their ethnic integrity but lacked the political power for change.

The situation finally did change in the 1970s, when Congress determined that Spanish-speaking children require some instruction in their own language. Charitably, one might say that the new policy was intended to cut down the high dropout rate among Hispanics, and thus to reduce Hispanic unemployment. Or, one could argue that the Hispanic minority—then about 5 or 6 percent and growing fast—commanded enough votes to make the change politically wise. In either event, Spanish became a second language of instruction, though everyone agrees that Hispanic children have to learn English as well.

The minimum competency tests now raise disturbing new questions about bilingual education. So far, the tests have been only in English. A few states exempt narrowly defined classes of multilingual students (Gorth and Perkins 1979). But still, despite all the funding and "commitment" to bilingual education out front, we have sneaked in the old policy by the back door. Just as before, many students not fluent in English by the time they graduate will be denied full participation in American society.

Setting up fluency in English as a diploma requirement may or may not be a good idea; there are arguments both ways, which I am not about to examine here. We must, however, recognize that the schools are once again giving with one hand and taking away with the other. Either Spanish has become a second American tongue, alongside English, or it has not. If it has, then students should be allowed to demonstrate their competency in Spanish. If it has not, then we are systematically dooming people to massive unemployment, even in trades and neighborhoods where fluent English is not especially helpful. This is hardly a satisfactory result, for it will only exacerbate the social problems we see today wherever there is high unemployment in particular geographic areas. Thus, we must either improve instruction in English to the point where nearly all Spanish-speaking students can pass the competency tests, or else offer the tests in Spanish as well. The injustice to Hispanic students in the meantime is too great.

The same injustice, in slightly different form, affects students who speak native languages other than English or Spanish. In generations past, an immigrant could achieve a good life with very little education, and often without much English. That is no longer as true as it used to be; the lack of a high school diploma is now an almost insurmountable handicap, one that can influence generations. My own grandfather arrived from Romania in 1904 with little education, no money, and no way to communicate, yet he had a large and thriving business when he finally retired. His son, my father, finished college, probably the first among his ancestors to do so. His success enabled me, in turn, to go through graduate school and take a place in the professions. Such stories were commonplace in decades past but there may be far fewer of them in the future. If my grandfather immigrated today, his lack of education would be far more likely to transmit itself to his children and grandchildren because the opportunities for him to get started without an education would be scarce.

We have, in short, reverted to the policy of learn-English-or-drop-out, through the minimum competency tests. And dropping out is not what it used to be: Most jobs are closed to young people who lack a diploma. The result is a severe penalty on children with the bad judgment to pick non-English-speaking parents.

For handicapped students, the situation is even worse than it is for the racial and linguistic minorities. Although there is often little question as to the person's ability to meet a minimum competency standard, some handicaps can make it very difficult to display that ability. And once more, the schools are acting inconsistently. In passing the Education for All Handicapped Children Act of 1975,[5] Congress placed handicapped children in ordinary classrooms, to the extent possible. "Least restrictive environment" is the operative phrase. In about half the competency states handicapped students take the same minimum competency test as their classmates and are held to the same standards (Gorth and Perkins 1979). The same test on paper may be a very different test to the student, depending on the handicap involved. Again the schools made a promise that the tests require them to break.

Despite the common tendency to think of them as a group, handicapped children vary widely. They have all the variation of nonhandicapped children, plus the added diversity of their very different handicaps. In testing, the precise nature and extent of the handicap are extremely important. A student confined to a wheelchair, for example, may be at no particular disadvantage. For one who lacks the full use of his writing hand, an amanuensis will reduce the disadvantage to insignificance. But what of a student who is blind? It is practically impossible to devise a test comparable to that for a sighted student. Florida offers its exam in large print and Braille. But that, or even having someone read the questions aloud (as in some states), does not help much. A sighted person can compare the multiple-choice alternatives at a glance, which is very different from having them presented slowly and serially. And any but the simplest mathematics problem is all but impossible for someone who must work and remember every step in his head.

Testing difficulties only touch the real problem, however. More important is whether handicapped students' education prior to the test can be properly equated to that of their classmates and fairly tested to the same standards. Consider a student who is blind, or deaf, or dyslexic. Despite a school's best efforts, there is simply no way to provide an "educational opportunity" for that student that matches what is available to others. The student's condition rules it out from the start.

Still, the minimum competency states must take responsibility for handicapped students in one way or another. Their worst option is to treat handicapped students the same as everyone else: to give them the same test and hold them to the same standards. The result, inevitably, will be some students who fail to receive a diploma solely because their handicap makes performance on the test impossible, even though they possess the requisite skills. This option is not only unfair, but possibly illegal as well. The Rehabilitation Act of 1973 provides that "No otherwise qualified handicapped individual in the United States . . . shall, solely by reason of his handicap . . . be denied the benefits of . . . any program or activity receiving federal assistance."[6] Although the question has not yet been litigated, the courts may well find that a diploma, otherwise properly earned, is a "benefit" not to be denied for reason of handicap. The handicapped student, accordingly, would be in an excellent position to bring suit.

Even changes in the form of the test may not be enough to compensate for students' handicaps, as we have seen. McClung and Pullin (1978, p. 924) list three main policies that school systems could adopt, assuming cosmetic accommodations such as tests in Braille:

1. Holding handicapped students to the same standards as others and issuing the same diploma to those who pass;

2. Setting up different standards for handicapped students, presumably less demanding, and still issuing the same diploma;

3. Setting up different standards but issuing a different diploma to match.

The third option may run afoul of the statute quoted above if the student can show that the lesser diploma comes solely because of his or her handicap. That would not be hard to prove. And the second choice might be challenged by nonhandicapped students who fail their own more stringent standards, on the grounds that they are being discriminated against for their lack of a handicap. The outcome of such a suit, it should be noted, is more uncertain than one brought by a handicapped student under the statute; the courts have not been sympathetic so far to claims of "reverse discrimination." The first option, of course, is open to challenge under the statute.

Any policy that distinguishes among students with and without handicaps will be subject to problems in practice. Wherever one puts the margin, there are always marginal cases. A great many handicaps are marginal in themselves—partially defective vision, for example, or a minor speech impediment like a lisp. Others, though definitely impediments, are hard to diagnose reliably. Many learning disabilities fall in this category. Yet a minimum competency procedure that makes any special allowances for handicapped students will need some reasonably certain way to identify that group. Doing so opens the possibility of a Pandora's box of students vying to be placed on one side of the line or the other. (The Education for All Handicapped Children Act outlines procedures for determining who is handicapped, but for a very different end — federal aid to education, not fairness in standards for testing.)

There is also a political complication. Some school systems, to attract federal funding, seek to identify as many students as possible with relatively minor handicaps. Whenever a child stumbles over a word, somebody yells "Dyslexia!" and goes running for a therapist. The effect is an artificial inflation, in some areas, in the numbers of handicapped. Other areas underreport, also for financial reasons. The indiscriminate labeling can cause trouble later, when it comes time to test. Students whose handicaps might not have been noticed at all, save for the federal and state funding programs, may demand preferential treatment, and others whose handicaps went carefully unseen might want the benefit of less stringent standards.

Most people who have thought about the problem, including McClung and Pullin (1978), recommend making individual decisions about who is handicapped and about the extent of appropriate departures from the ordinary testing procedures in each case. This has a sensible ring to it, but the suggestion simply shifts the problem from one setting to another, from a rule-making body to the principal's office. And even at this level, school staff members need guidelines that they can apply to individual cases. Otherwise the whole procedure will become arbitrary and capricious. Yet developing such guidelines presents almost the same problems as developing formal rules.

The central difficulty, of course, is the same one that makes almost every other aspect of minimum competency testing so hard to administer fairly. Children are different from one another, and any attempt to treat them uniformly is certain to cause injustice, at least in some cases. A child whose home environment makes peaceful study impossible is "handicapped" in school as surely as a certified dyslexic (perhaps even more so than a paraplegic whose teachers and parents are supportive), yet has no protection from his disadvantage in the testing process. A student in fear of his physical safety on the streets, or dealing with a pregnancy, or in trouble with drugs, or sought by the police cannot attend to learning with a clear mind. A physical or mental handicap, in short, is only one kind of barrier that a student might have to overcome. If a handicap merits sympathetic regard from the schools, then perhaps some of the other barriers do as well.

The schools cannot possibly delve into every student's personal life and set individual competency standards accordingly. Yet something of the sort is the only way to impose fairly, on a diverse student group, the supposedly uniform standards that minimum competency testing seeks to enforce. Accordingly, with education as we operate it today, there is no way to set a fair competency test. Standards that are uniform in principle are anything but uniform in practice.

The problem is especially clear among minority and handicapped students but applies with equal force to almost everyone. Every child is a minority of one. Every child has handicaps, if we apply the term broadly, just as every child with an "official" handicap has his own particular strengths. Until the schools are prepared to meet every student where he stands, a competency test that can threaten the product of twelve years of a child's life is unfair, unjust, and possibly illegal as well.

Notes

1. Paul F-Brandwein, who has held various academic posts in science and education and was formerly vice-chairman of Harcourt Brace Jovanovich, is now director of research for that publishing company. In a personal communication, Brandwein told me that he first used the expression in 1952 but believes that he heard it from B. Frank Brown, then principal of Melbourne High School, Florida. Brandwein provided me with a monograph in which he used the expression in this sense: "We are about to realize that there is nothing so unequal as the equal treatment of unequals — unequals in experience, history, and previous opportunity. In the coming years — no matter how long it takes — we will give each individual his or her due" (Brandwein 1971).

2. Television set-aside portion of the Emergency School Aid Act, 20 U.S.C. §§3194 (b) (2), 3202.

3. Elementary and Secondary Education Acts, 20 U.S.C. §§241a *et seq*.

4. Florida, for example, provides data that are more trustworthy than most, having been accepted as evidence in the federal courts. "Between October 1977 and May 1979, the number of students who were in Florida public

high schools first as juniors and then as seniors had been reduced to 91,000 students. Of the approximately 91,000 high school seniors, 3,466 or 20.049% of the black students had not passed the test compared to 1,342 or 1.9% of the white students. The failure rate among black students was approximately 10 times that among white students." *Debra P. v. Turlington,* 474 F. Supp. 244, 249 (M.D. Fla. 1979).

    5. The act is also known as PL 94-142 and is codified at 20 U.S.C. §§1401 *et seq.* For the implementing regulations, see 45 C.F.R. 121(a).

    6. The quotation is from Section 504 of the Rehabilitation Act of 1973, 29 U.S.C. §794. Implementing regulations are at 45 C.F.R. 81, 84.

6

Legal Background of Minimum Competency Testing

M inimum competency testing has been the subject of debate for many years. By now, almost every educational institution has taken a stand—legislatures, state and local agencies, principals, teachers and their unions, parents, even, occasionally, students. Other factions in society have also expressed their views: liberals, conservatives, minorities, industry, labor, academia, and so on. The patchwork of approaches to competency testing that we see now, with almost as many variations as there are states, is a product of shifting compromises among many interested groups.

In all the clamor, however, there is one important voice—the courts—that has so far spoken but once. The courts will be a steadily growing influence in the future. Indeed, whether competency testing survives at all, and in what forms, may come to depend more on judicial decisions than on any other factor.

Jerrold Zacharias once observed that a university faculty, sitting as a body, "has all the brakes and none of the engines." The same could be said of the courts. A judge can rarely initiate new action; the separation of powers puts most of the engines in the legislative and executive branches. But the braking power of the courts is immense. A single judge can stop millions of people in their tracks if he finds the enterprise running counter to the laws and principles that the courts enforce. It is natural, then, that people who feel they have been wronged by competency testing will turn to the courts for help.

Many of the issues already raised in this book will reappear as the subject matter of lawsuits. These lawsuits may involve the tests' potential for racial and ethnic discrimination, the question of whether students have enough warning of the test as a diploma requirement, the tests' unfairness to handicapped students, the error inherent in all test results, and the problem of matching tests to curriculum. In Chapter 7, I will analyze a recent court decision on competency testing—the only one that has been handed down at this writing. The legal issues it addresses parallel some of the most often heard criticisms of competency testing. But when the criticism comes from a court, it can carry the force of law.

No court action springs from a vacuum, even in a case that is the very first of its kind. Prior decisions nearly always influence the outcome. Accordingly, it will be useful to begin with some discussion of certain background issues, and the legal cases deciding them, that are especially likely to have an impact on the developing body of law on minimum competency testing.

Direct legal action on minimum competency testing has been sparse because there has not been time for it, yet. The courts cannot step in until someone complains of being harmed; and although the tests have been used in some states for years, their scores have only recently begun to affect students' lives directly. It is only when the competency test phase-in periods have ended in the various states, only when diplomas begin to be withheld from students, that any judicial action can be taken. It is only now, in the early 1980s, that the tests are making enough of a concrete change that students can begin to bring suit.

A school system cannot ask a court, "If we did so-and-so and a student sued, how would you rule?" Nor can students sue in advance, in case they might not receive their diplomas. In order for the courts to become involved, there must be an actual dispute, a "present controversy," not just a theoretical question. And even where there has been actual harm, the courts cannot take an interest until the people involved bring the issue forward. In the words of Dean John Kramer of Georgetown University Law Center, "The courts do not ride the range in search of injustice."

With only one competency testing case having gone through trial to a decision, the law is still largely unsettled. Other cases are now moving through the judicial pipeline, so the law should become much clearer over the next several years. But in the meantime, some of the individual issues that are most likely to arise have been ruled on in other settings. These cases offer the best available guide to future decisions on minimum competency testing.

There is potential for a new kind of social wrong in competency testing, a species of harm unknown in the past.[1] Such new matters receive special attention in the courts because later cases will look to these first decisions for guidance. New questions can also be difficult to decide because the judges hearing them have little specific precedent to follow.

Even so, the courts prefer not to make new law out of whole cloth. Ordinarily that is a task for the legislatures. A high appeals court will overturn all precedent once in a while, when justice demands it, and overrule past decisions in light of changing conditions. But most of the time, a judge ruling on a new question would rather "find the law" in past decisions. Thus, a new situation requires the judge to look for analogies in other, related areas of the law. The court will try to apply the reasoning of its predecessors in other kinds of cases to the case at hand. The analogies sometimes seem strained, but the practice lends some predictability to new areas of the law.

In minimum competency, two older kinds of cases are most likely to supply this kind of influence. In a handful of actions in "educational malpractice," illiterate high school graduates have sued their school systems for failing to educate them properly.[2] Typically, the child sought the money he would be unable to earn in the future due to his lack of skills. So far all of these suits have failed, each time in a flood of publicity. The reasons for their failure, which I shall examine shortly, may bear on future minimum competency decisions.

The second sequence of cases that may apply deals with the question of unlawful discrimination by race. This issue is better established, having come before the U.S. Supreme Court several times. As the competency requirements fall harder on blacks than on whites, discrimination suits are likely to result. And in any action that alleges discrimination, past Supreme Court decisions are likely to become part of the analysis.[3]

Indeed, the one case already ruled upon, *Debra P. v. Turlington,*[4] involved charges of discrimination. We shall look at this case in some detail in the next chapter. Discrimination was established; the students won. Yet both sides claimed victory: the students because the state was prohibited from withholding diplomas on the basis of minimum competency tests for four years, and the state because the test itself emerged unscathed. The case has been appealed,[5] and future cases like it are inevitable.

Educational Malpractice

The decisions on educational malpractice—there have been only four or five in the whole country—concern a school's responsibility to educate its students. This issue has obvious implications for minimum competency. To follow the implications, however, we shall have to examine the legal background of these suits and take a close look at how the judges framed their opinions.

A suit for educational malpractice is one example of what lawyers call a "tort action." Crudely defined, a "tort" is a civil wrong that does not involve a contract. The most common torts nowadays are probably those arising in automobile accidents, where one driver sues another for injuries or damage to his car. Cases of medical and legal malpractice are tort suits. Someone who slips on a piece of lettuce in the supermarket and is injured in the fall might also sue on a tort.

Tort cases have a long history in the law. Over the centuries, the courts have developed firm guidelines for handling them. Though a tort always rests on one person having wronged another, the harm itself is not enough to constitute a tort. In order for the courts to act, the wrong and its surrounding circumstances must also fit into the legal rules that define a tort.

The rules vary somewhat among the states, but in most

jurisdictions the plaintiff—the person suing—must prove these four elements:

1. That the defendant—the person whom he is suing—owed the plaintiff a duty of care;

2. That the defendant was negligent in performing that duty;

3. That the plaintiff was injured—but not necessarily in body, for the injury can also be financial, to reputation, etc.;

4. That the negligence more or less directly caused the injury.

(In some states the plaintiff must also prove that he did not contribute to the injury by being negligent himself, but that is not a factor in the cases we shall consider here.)

In educational malpractice, there is no question as to injury, the third element of a tort. A student who graduates from high school unable to read or write will be disadvantaged throughout life. And the fourth element is also satisfied, for a student's illiteracy has to be at least partly the school's fault—especially, as sometimes happens, when the school seemed unaware that the student was having trouble. In that situation, there can be little doubt as to the school's negligence, the second element.

Nevertheless, all educational malpractice cases so far have failed. The obstacle each time has been the first element, the question of whether it is the school's duty to educate the student. It surprised many people to learn that such a duty does not exist in the law. But as we shall see, the courts had to clarify the notion of "duty" in order to arrive at this conclusion.

The first and best known of the educational malpractice cases was *Peter W. v. San Francisco Unified School District.*[6] (In the lower court the plaintiff was called "Peter Doe," and most newspaper accounts have used that name.) Peter claimed that he graduated from high school with a fifth-grade reading ability, an education that fit him only for manual labor. The school failed to detect his reading problems and correct them, he said, and so was negligent in its duty.

In response, the school system argued (in effect) that even if all the facts that Peter alleged were true, he still had no legal right to collect. That is, even if Peter was in fact illiterate due to the school system's negligence, said the school system, it still did not owe him damages. The judge agreed and dismissed the case without a trial. As Peter would have lost the case even if he could prove his claims at trial, there was no point in having the trial. Peter appealed, claiming that the lower court had misapplied the law.

The appeals court, however, went along with the lower court. In its written opinion the appeals court began:

> The novel — and troublesome — question on this appeal is whether a person who claims to have been inadequately educated, while a student in a public school system, may state a cause of action in tort against the public authorities who operate and administer the system. We hold that he may not.[7]

Thus the decision in this case, as in all the educational malpractice cases that followed, turned on the question of whether Peter's claim constituted a tort. The quality of education has never become an issue in these cases because the courts have always been able to make their decisions without dealing with that question. It is as if one person sued another for making a rude gesture. The court could perfectly well conclude that a rude gesture does not constitute a tort, and thereby dismiss the case — without ever considering the question of whether the gesture in fact was made.

After disposing of some preliminary matters, the court's opinion considered the elements of a tort, much as they appear in the numbered list above. Only the first element came into dispute — whether a school has a "duty of care" to the student for his education. Certainly the school has that duty, said the court, but the duty is not necessarily a legal duty:

> Of course, no reasonable observer would be heard to say that these facts did not impose upon [the school system] a "duty of care" within any common meaning of the term; given the commanding importance of public education in society, we state a truism in remarking that the public authorities who are dutybound to educate are also bound to do it with "care." But the truism does not answer the present inquiry, in which "duty of care" is not a term of common parlance; it is instead a legalistic concept of

"duty" which will sustain liability for negligence in its breach, and it must be analyzed in that light.[8]

What determines whether the duty of care here is not merely a moral duty, but a legal duty as well? Pointing to several earlier cases, the court concluded this to be a question of "public policy." The mention of public policy in an opinion usually signals that the court plans to look beyond the facts of the case before it and to take into account the long-range consequences of its decision, as best it can foresee them.

To find a legal duty in the *Peter W.* case would bring the case squarely within tort law and would thus make the schools liable for malpractice. The possibility of many such suits was anticipated by the court. Such suits would have considerable impact on the public, because a great many illiterate students might then recover substantial damages from public funds.

The court, by raising the issue of public policy, turned the question around. That is, it did *not* determine whether the schools have a legal duty to educate, in order to see if the schools are liable. Instead, it asked—in order to decide whether there is a legal duty to educate—whether making the schools liable is a good idea. To say there is no legal duty of care, in other words, becomes a shorthand way of saying it would simply be bad policy to hold the schools liable for failing to educate.[9]

This kind of argument sounds contrived, to say the least. Why can't the court just rule against Peter and be done with it? If it did that, however, a great deal of tort law in California would lose its underpinning. People there could no longer be certain whether the traditional torts still applied. By shoehorning its opinion into the established rules, the court left the rest of the law unchanged so that people could plan their affairs accordingly.

Another main reason for the court's conclusion, in addition to taxpayer expense, is the difficulty of laying the blame on the proper people. When a student does not learn, said the court, there is no way to tell whether the failure is due to malpractice or to other causes instead:

Unlike the activity of the highway or the marketplace, classroom

methodology affords no readily acceptable standards of care, or
cause, or injury. The science of pedagogy itself is fraught with
different and conflicting theories of how or what a child should
be taught, and any layman might — and commonly does — have
his own emphatic views on the subject. The "injury" claimed
here is plaintiff's inability to read and write. Substantial professional authority attests that the achievement of literacy in the
schools, or its failure, are influenced by a host of factors which
affect the pupil subjectively, from outside the formal teaching
process, and beyond the control of its ministers. They may be
physical, neurological, emotional, cultural, environmental; they
may be present but not perceived, recognized but not
identified.[10]

This passage has been widely quoted in the educational
literature. Understandably, school people find it comforting.
No doubt it will be quoted again in minimum competency suits,
in the briefs for defending school systems. At least in California, this passage goes a long way toward exonerating the schools
from any educational failure.

In the minimum competency setting, however, this argument
raises an interesting question. A failing student could well ask,
"If education is so chancy a business as the court says it is, how
can the schools ever set fair standards for students to meet?"
Note the factors to which the court pointed, all of them possibly
unperceived and possibly unidentified. The court excused the
school because these factors are "beyond the control of its
ministers." But these same factors are completely beyond the
student's control as well. In the *Peter W.* case, the court was
willing to let the damage remain where it fell, on the student. In
a minimum competency case, however, might a court use the
same argument to excuse the student? In terms of policy, it
seems just as unfair to hold the student responsible for his
failure to learn as it does to blame the school, if the factors that
prevent learning are indeed beyond the reach of both.

The court's opinion went on to spell out how being subject to
tort suits like this one would place a massive financial burden on
the public schools. To those who have followed the rise of
minimum competency testing, the thought will strike a familiar
chord:

Few of our institutions, if any, have aroused the controversies, or incurred the public dissatisfaction, which have attended the operation of the public schools during the last few decades. Rightly or wrongly, but widely, they are charged with outright failure in the achievement of their educational objectives; according to some critics, they bear responsibility for many of the social and moral problems of our society at large. . . . To hold them to an actionable "duty of care," in the discharge of their academic functions, would expose them to the tort claims—real or imagined—of disaffected students and parents in countless numbers. . . . The ultimate consequences, in terms of public time and money, would burden them—and society—beyond calculation.[11]

The reasoning here does not seem consistent with simple logic. The court said: Because a lot of people have lost confidence in the schools, the schools need protection against possible lawsuits. (Note the reluctance to take sides on whether the loss of confidence is justified.) Can we conclude that if people generally were happier with the schools, then an occasional malcontent could bring suit? On the face of it, it would seem more logical to hold the schools liable *especially* when their clients are widely dissatisfied. Otherwise, as far as malpractice is concerned, the schools gain every legal advantage by doing a poor job.

Yet the court's conclusion is necessary, as a practical matter. Logic and wishful thinking aside, it is a fact that malpractice liability could cripple the educational system. The present climate would lead to a great number of malpractice suits. Their financial consequences would leave the schools incapable of surviving in anything like their present form. The court ruled as it had to.

The financial burden argument is worth remembering when students who fail the competency exams start bringing suit for financial damages. Some students will probably argue that their failure to earn a diploma is due to the school's negligence. Some will seek financial compensation for wages lost due to lack of a diploma. Such suits are unlikely to succeed, if the courts continue to follow the reasoning in *Peter W*. That would be an ironic result, however: The same public disaffection with the schools that promoted the imposition of standards, through the competency movement, leads the court to protect the school from its own failure to meet those same standards.

Peter W. complained, among other things, that he had received a diploma in spite of his illiteracy and so was deprived of further public instruction. This is a curious twist on the more probable suits over minimum competency, where students will complain of *not* being granted a diploma. Indeed, had California been a diploma-withholding state when this suit arose, Peter W. could not have sued on quite the same grounds that he did.[12]

Let us suppose, for the sake of discussion, that the San Francisco school system had indeed administered a minimum competency test to Peter W., watched him fail, and then denied him a diploma. Peter sues, let us say, for lack of an education as he did before, but also for lack of the diploma. How might the suit turn out?

According to attorney Merle McClung, Peter's failing the test might actually give him a better case. "The lack of objective standards in education," says McClung, "is one reason why no educational malpractice case of this kind has ever been successful."[13] McClung is referring specifically to the *Peter W.* case and to a New York case we shall look at presently. He explains his reasoning in a later publication:

> Competency testing programs, with their relatively objective measures of competence, may have inadvertently strengthened the educational malpractice claim. Unlike the education programs involved in *Peter W.,* . . . competency testing programs attempt to set clearly specified standards. . . . Whether such standards would strengthen some educational malpractice claims sufficiently to prevail remains an open question (McClung 1980).

Yet there is much in the *Peter W.* opinion that a minimum competency test, objective standards and all, would leave unchanged. Indeed, the court's two other arguments seem sufficient to support the decision: the host of factors outside the school's control, and the forecast of costs to society if failing students could sue. The question of standards, though mentioned in the opinion, does not appear essential to the outcome.

A lower court in California would have a hard time awarding money damages to a student in light of *Peter W.,* even if the student were denied a diploma. It could be done; judges have gone against stronger precedent in the past. But if the student were simply suing for his diploma, and not for money, it would be a different matter. Among other distinctions, such a case would not have to meet the standards for a tort at all. We shall look at an example of such a case in the next chapter.

Outside the state of California, the *Peter W.* ruling is useful advice to the courts but is not controlling. A few states have issued similar opinions, though with nothing like the useful analysis that Justice Rattigan set forth in *Peter W.* Accordingly, the outcome of future litigation in other jurisdictions is harder to predict.

New York State's case is *Donohue v. Copiague Union Free School District.*[14] The facts were very similar to those in *Peter W.* Donohue, too, received a diploma despite his lack of skills. And again, the court dismissed the case without a trial, agreeing with the school system that the student could not win even if he proved all of his allegations to be true. The dismissal was affirmed on two consecutive appeals. It is the third and final ruling that we consider here, handed down by the highest court in New York State.

In the *Donohue* case, the court did not mention the question of financial burden. Moreover, it disagreed with the *Peter W.* court on the question of standards by which to judge malpractice, finding that standards might be feasible after all:

If doctors, lawyers, architects, engineers and other professionals are charged with a duty owing to the public whom they serve, it could be said that nothing in the law precludes similar treatment of professional educators. Nor would creation of a standard with which to judge an educator's performance of that duty necessarily pose an insurmountable obstacle. As for proximate causation [i.e., that the negligence and not something else caused the injury], while this element might indeed be difficult, if not impossible, to prove in view of the many collateral factors involved in the learning process, it perhaps assumes too much to conclude that it could never be established.[15]

The *Donohue* court thus ignored one of the *Peter W.* arguments, that of financial burden, and disagreed with the other two arguments, those on standards and the difficulty of placing blame. Its opinion does not even mention the *Peter W.* case.[16] In finding for the school system, the *Donohue* court relied on two new arguments. The less important argument concerned the availability in New York State of administrative procedures, outside the court system, through which citizens can press educational complaints. More significant, however, was the court's fear of becoming too deeply involved in the educational process:

> To entertain a cause of action for "educational malpractice" [i.e., to allow a suit for it] would require the courts not merely to make judgments as to the validity of broad educational policies—a course we have unalteringly eschewed in the past—but, more importantly, to sit in review of the day-to-day implementation of these policies. Recognition in the courts of this cause of action would constitute blatant interference with the responsibility for the administration of the public school system lodged by Constitution and statute in school administrative agencies.[17]

This argument against "blatant interference" may apply with equal force to minimum competency suits. The courts have always been reluctant to take part in administering schools—or anything else—on a continuing basis. There are exceptions, such as the District Court's close involvement in desegregating the Boston schools. But for the most part, a court would rather make a ruling that requires no further attention, if it can do so fairly. And a court will prefer not to hand down a decision that it cannot enforce. This apparently was a concern in the *Donohue* ruling. The payment of damages to Donohue himself is simple enough, but the case would have set a precedent. To do justice in subsequent suits, the court would have to establish guidelines for the schools on their legal duty to educate and then monitor those guidelines. This it was not prepared to do.

In our hypothetical tort suit for money damages by a student denied his diploma, exactly the same problems might arise if the student won the case. The schools would be entitled to a clear statement from the courts as to how they should proceed in order to avoid losing in subsequent litigation. (In much the same way, a supermarket held liable when a shopper slips on a piece of lettuce will want to know what standards of maintenance the court considers adequate so it can protect itself in the future.) A ruling against the schools in a minimum competency suit could thus involve the court in the details of education, an outcome the *Donohue* decision sought to avoid.

A court will, nevertheless, assume this kind of responsibility when it sees no other just solution. That was apparently the case in Boston desegregation decisions. And if a court determines that a minimum competency case has the appropriate significance—for example, if far-reaching constitutional issues are at stake—it might well take on a continuing involvement with the educational system as the price of doing justice.

Racial Discrimination in the Schools

When constitutional issues do arise in competency testing, it will most likely be in the context of discrimination. One such case, *Debra P. v. Turlington,*[18] has already been judged partly on constitutional grounds. The many Supreme Court cases on discrimination, though not concerned with competency testing as such, will have an important influence on any such future litigation. The law on discrimination has not yet been fully settled, and attorneys will be watching the emerging patterns closely. Here, I shall review four of the leading cases to date. These cases raise some of the issues likely to predominate in disputes over minimum competency testing.

The landmark case in educational discrimination is still *Brown v. Board of Education,*[19] which in 1954 required nationwide desegregation of public schools. In its opinion, the U.S. Supreme Court reaffirmed the state's obligation to provide an adequate education for every student:

Today, education is perhaps the most important function of state and local governments. Compulsory school attendance laws and the great expenditures for education both demonstrate our recognition of the importance of education to our democratic society. It is required in the performance of our most basic public responsibilities, even service in the armed forces. It is the very foundation of good citizenship. Today it is a principal instrument in awakening the child to cultural values, in preparing him for later professional training, and in helping him to adjust normally to his environment. In these days, it is doubtful that any child may reasonably be expected to succeed in life if he is denied the opportunity of an education. Such an opportunity, where the state has undertaken to provide it, is a right which must be made available to all on equal terms.[20]

In the next paragraph were the words that changed at a stroke the face of education in the United States.

We come then to the question presented: Does segregation of children in public schools solely on the basis of race, even though the physical facilities and other "tangible" factors may be equal, deprive the children of the minority group of equal educational opportunities? We believe that it does.[21]

The *Brown* decision is an important precursor to the minimum competency movement, especially where it speaks of a right to education "which must be made available to all on equal terms." Unless educational opportunities are equal, competency testing with its sanctions would be unconscionable. The Supreme Court, in the *Brown* opinion, set down one of the requirements for equal opportunity, that of educational facilities integrated by race. Regardless of their other qualities, segregated facilities were held to be inherently unequal. It was on this very basic point that the *Debra P.* court struck down competency testing in Florida, for a limited time at least.

Brown, of course, triggered a public outcry and a flood of litigation. The courts have been busy ever since, applying *Brown's* seemingly simple rule to a broad range of school settings and situations. During the same period, the discrimination controversy also involved questions outside of education. In some of these cases, the results affected education nonetheless.

One such dispute, very influential in later discrimination cases, dealt with pre-employment testing—the closest that the Supreme Court has come, so far, to anything resembling the minimum competency question. *Washington v. Davis*[22] involved a suit brought by two black men rejected as recruits by the police force in Washington, D.C. (The "Washington" in the case name refers to the mayor at that time, Walter Washington, not to the city.) The two men claimed they were turned down because of a "written personnel test which excluded a disproportionately high number of Negro applicants."[23] They argued that use of the test violated constitutional equal-protection guarantees as well as various statutes.

The Court faced an interesting dilemma. There was no reason to think that the city was discriminating on purpose; on the contrary, the city was energetically trying, through an affirmative action plan, to attract more blacks to the police force. Yet the test unquestionably screened out more blacks than whites.

Had the discrimination been deliberate, the Court would have had an easier time. As it was, though, the Court had to decide whether inadvertent discrimination — that is, discrimination that comes as a side effect of some other process — is contrary to the Constitution. This same question, of course, is certain to come up in suits over the competency question.

At the outset, the Court in *Washington v. Davis* had to determine whether the test itself was valid. If it was not, then its use was discriminatory, and there would have been little more to say about it. Evaluating tests, as we have seen, is never a simple matter. And in this instance, where test quality could govern the outcome of the case, the parties could not even agree on what standards to use in measuring the test.

Three standards were proposed. The plaintiffs pointed out that Title VII of the Civil Rights Act forbids use of a test with discriminatory impact unless the test can satisfy a formal validation. This is a very difficult standard to meet. Citing the complex guidelines recommended by the American Psychological Association, the Court found the standards too rigorous for a constitutional case. (Even though a test might fail to satisfy Title VII, it can still fall within constitutional limits. But if it were the other way around and the test satisfied a statute but not the Constitution, then the statute would be unconstitutional. A statute may be stricter than the Constitution, but it may not be more lax.)

Thus the Court took a view more pragmatic than that of Title VII and asked simply whether the test predicted success in the police force. But success in what? In the training program, or in later performance on the job? The distinction is critical because tests given before training are notoriously poor at predicting the quality of work later on, during actual employment. Even the much-touted Law School Admissions Test makes no claims for success in law, but only for success in law school—and just the first year of law school, at that. Here, the Court settled again for the easier standard. Finding that the test did predict success in the training program, it pronounced the test satisfactory.

Again, this issue presents something of an analogy to the competency testing situation. In Chapter 1, I noted the distinction between assessing a student's learning in school subjects and his acquisition of skills for daily life. There are at least three standards for judging competency tests more or less parallel to the standards considered in *Washington v. Davis:* formal validation studies as recommended by the American Psychological Association; less formal predictions of success in adult pursuits (analagous to success on the police force); and correlations with other measures of achievement in school (analagous to success in the police training program). It would be a mistake to push these analogies too far. The lower courts, however, may find in *Washington v. Davis* a suggestion that they can hold a test acceptable if it seems to fulfill some socially useful purpose. For a minimum competency test, this might require simply showing that the test coincides with educational objectives. Even if the test falls short of stricter standards, and even though it discriminates by race, it may still be able to meet the constitutional requirements.

We now return to the discrimination issue. Some earlier cases in the lower courts of appeals had looked no further than discriminatory effects, holding procedures to be unconstitutional simply because they fell harder on blacks than on whites. The Supreme Court took the opportunity in *Washington v. Davis* to reject that view: A law or official act is not unconstitutional *solely* because it has a racially disproportionate impact. That is, a discriminatory test is not automatically unconstitutional. But the Court also drew a second boundary: A socially useful test is not automatically constitutional, either. "A statute, otherwise neutral on its face," said the Court, "must not be applied so as invidiously to discriminate on the basis of race."[24]

The Court seemed to be saying that discriminatory impact is acceptable as long as it is not "invidious." But isn't discrimination by its nature invidious? And if not, then what makes one act of discrimination invidious and another constitutional? Justice White, writing for the majority, approached the first question with some care:

> [T]he discriminatory impact . . . may for all practical purposes demonstrate unconstitutionality because in various circumstances the discrimination is very difficult to explain on nonracial grounds. Nevertheless, we have not held that a law, neutral on its face and serving ends otherwise within the power of government to pursue, is invalid under the Equal Protection Clause simply because it may affect a greater proportion of one race than of another. Disproportionate impact is not irrelevant, but it is not the sole touchstone of an invidious racial discrimination forbidden by the Constitution. Standing alone, it does not trigger the rule that racial classifications are to be subjected to the strictest scrutiny and are justifiable only by the weightiest of considerations.[25]

As for the second question, the Court maintained that what makes discrimination invidious, and therefore unconstitutional, is the intent that lies behind it. Deliberate discrimination is forbidden; discrimination that "just occurs," when the intent is otherwise, is acceptable as long as the law in question is neutral in its wording and serving a valid purpose. Motivation is the key to unconstitutionality in *Washington v. Davis*. The discriminatory impact, however, is part of the evidence of discriminatory intent. The distinction is a subtle one but turns out to be very important in later cases.

In other areas of the law, the courts have long ruled on the basis of people's intent—in cases of manslaughter, for example, and sometimes in tort actions. The courts regularly look to the "intent of the Congress" in construing statutes. But the courts have also recognized that intent, as a psychological state, is impossible to determine for certain by any means short of telepathy. Accordingly, "legal intent" is not quite the same thing as psychological intent. Legal intent is necessarily inferred from the facts of the situation, for there is no other objective way to arrive at it. The inference runs something like this: What would be the intention of a reasonable person who acted in such-and-such a way? Whether the person involved actually had that intent in mind is more or less beside the point, because his state of mind cannot be proved in court except by implication from his actions.

The issue of discriminatory intent thus becomes less mystical than it sounds. Putting it crudely, the question is merely whether the person who discriminated acted as if he meant to do so. In *Washington v. Davis,* the Court had little trouble in concluding that the discrimination was *not* intentional. Indeed, the two plaintiffs had never claimed that there was "intentional discrimination or purposeful discriminatory acts" against them,[26] but only that the test "bore no relationship to job performance and has a highly discriminatory impact in screening out black candidates."[27] No court is likely to find a wrongful intent when the plaintiffs themselves do not. Moreover, the Court took note of the city's affirmative action program as evidence that it did not intend to discriminate.

Justice Stevens, while concurring with the majority's outcome, had some reservations about setting up intent as the mark of unconstitutional discrimination. He noted the problems of determining an intent that is not borne out by actual events:

> Frequently the most probative evidence of intent will be objective evidence of what actually happened rather than evidence describing the subjective state of mind of the actor. For normally the actor is presumed to have intended the natural consequences of his deeds. . . . It is unrealistic, on the other hand, to require the victim of alleged discrimination to uncover the actual subjective intent of the decisionmaker.[28]

Note in Stevens's remark that the test of intent in *Washington v. Davis* puts a greater burden of proof on the victim. Before this case, all that a victim had to prove was discriminatory impact; but after *Washington v. Davis,* he or she must prove intent as well. A sympathetic court might not ask for much in the way of proof. But this change in the law unquestionably made unconstitutional discrimination harder to establish.

The issues raised in this case, although they appear in a different setting, are similar in principle to much of what we can expect in competency litigation. The question of intent is likely to figure prominently when more blacks than whites are denied high school diplomas in the future. The case also illustrates how the courts are likely to approach the competency situation, i.e., looking beyond the test results to weigh the tests against the social purposes that they are meant to serve. *Washington v. Davis* has been much cited in later discrimination suits; it is an important structural element in the current law.

There are two other influential cases that we can examine more briefly. Both cases apply the principles of *Washington v. Davis* to dissimilar situations and in the process help to pin down the elusive question of intent. In both cases, the plaintiffs failed to prove discriminatory intent to the Court's satisfaction.

The first that we shall look at, *Village of Arlington Heights v. Metropolitan Housing Corp.,*[29] was a zoning dispute. Arlington Heights, outside Chicago, had refused to rezone certain land for the construction of integrated apartment housing to be occupied by people of low and medium income. Local zoning codes restricted apartments to buffer neighborhoods between industrial and single-family areas, and the proposed site did not fit that requirement. Village residents, moreover, feared a drop in property values if the apartments were built.

There was no question that the existing zoning arrangements had discriminatory impact. As a practical matter, they effectively excluded blacks from Arlington Heights. But was there discriminatory intent, as required under *Washington v. Davis*? The Court also noted that even if the village had motives other than discrimination, it still might have been acting with discriminatory intent. A legislature typically acts out of many competing purposes. But if one of its motives is to discriminate, then the others will not make up a sufficient excuse. The same will be true, presumably, in competency testing.

Again, as in *Washington v. Davis,* the Court acknowledged that discriminatory impact was an important factor, a starting point in the investigation. But other factors that the Court looked for and did not find included: discrimination as a motivating factor in the zoning plans, specific events in the development of the plan that might point to discriminatory intent, departures from the usual sequence of procedures in drawing up these particular plans, any changes from the usual factors that the village considers in making its zoning decisions, and evidence in the record of debates and reports—the legislative history—that might suggest a discriminatory motive.

The Court determined that intent was lacking under all of these tests. (A cynic might find in this opinion a blueprint for discriminating and getting away with it.) One key point in the village's favor was that the zoning plans, including the buffer policy, had been in effect long before the controversy arose. Had the village waited until it foresaw black families moving in before ruling out the apartments on the proposed site, the outcome in *Arlington Heights* might have been quite different. But as it was, the Court found no difficulty in concluding,

> [The plaintiffs] simply failed to carry their burden of proving that discriminatory purpose was a motivating factor in the Village's decision.[30]

Still another case that can be expected to bear on competency litigation is *Personnel Administrator of Massachusetts v. Feeney,*[31] in which the most recent Supreme Court explanations of discriminatory intent appear. In Massachusetts, the state government has long hired and promoted veterans over nonveterans. Several other states have similar laws. When Feeney brought suit, over 98 percent of the veterans in Massachusetts were male. As a practical matter, then, the preference law operated overwhelmingly in favor of men. Feeney, as a woman and a nonveteran, found her chances for advancement in the state government seriously impeded by the law. After watching several less qualified veterans, all men, promoted ahead of her, she charged the state with sex discrimination.

Justice Stewart for the majority reiterated the principle of *Washington v. Davis:*

Most laws classify, and many affect certain groups unevenly, even though the law itself treats them no differently from all other members of the class described by the law. When the basic classification is rationally based, uneven effects upon particular groups within a class are ordinarily of no constitutional concern. The calculus of effects, the manner in which a particular law reverberates in a society, is a legislative and not a judicial responsibility. In assessing an equal protection challenge, a court is called upon only to measure the basic validity of the legislative classification.[32]

Two classifications immediately suspect, however, are those based directly on race or sex:

A racial classification, regardless of purported motivation, is presumptively invalid and can be upheld only upon an extraordinary justification.[33]

And elsewhere,

[A]ny state law overtly or covertly designed to prefer males over females in public employment would require an exceedingly persuasive justification to withstand a constitutional challenge under the Equal Protection Clause of the Fourteenth Amendment.[34]

Yet in this particular case, the Court held that Massachusetts has a legitimate interest in maintaining its long-standing veterans-preference statute. The validity of that interest means that the law is without discriminatory intent and is therefore constitutional, even though it works to the disadvantage of women. In so holding, the Court clarified an important element in the question of intent:

"Discriminatory purpose," however, implies more than intent as volition or intent as awareness of consequences. It implies that the decisionmaker, in this case a state legislature, selected or reaffirmed a particular course of action at least in part "because of," not merely "in spite of," its adverse effects upon an identifiable group.[35]

Perhaps thinking of Stevens's remark in the *Davis* case — that the actor is presumed to have intended the consequences of his deeds — Stewart added this footnote to the passage above:

> This is not to say that the inevitability or foreseeability of consequences of a neutral rule has no bearing upon the existence of discriminatory intent. Certainly, when the adverse consequences of a law upon an identifiable group are as inevitable as the gender-based consequences of [the Massachusetts veterans-preference statute], a strong inference that the adverse effects were desired can reasonably be drawn. . . . [Here] the inference simply fails to ripen into proof.[36]

In other words, Feeney had been unable to prove that the state's purposes in maintaining the statute were at least in part to discriminate against women. That would have been difficult to establish considering the statute's long history and its explicit allowances for women veterans and nurses.

The *Feeney* ruling establishes a difficult test, one that the courts will doubtless apply beyond sex discrimination to other forms of discrimination as well. Even if the plaintiff can show that an official act inevitably discriminates, that is not enough. He must also prove that the discrimination itself was a reason for the act. In many instances, the court will have to consider what other purposes the act might be meant to fulfill. Arguing that the other possible purposes do not apply, or are insufficient, will seldom be easy.

In the case of minimum competency, the *Feeney* test of intent will be a major hurdle. The required proof would amount to establishing that a state had instituted the competency test, and its diploma sanction, in order to deny minority students diplomas. Perhaps many people believe that to be true. But it will be difficult to prove in court. As long as the state can point to its legitimate interests in the testing program — and there are many it can name — the court is likely to find the discrimination acceptable under the *Feeney* ruling.

One remark in the *Feeney* opinion sums up the whole business fairly well: "[T]he Fourteenth Amendment guarantees equal laws, not equal results."[37] The remark does not say, however, just which laws must be equal in order that unequal results may stand. We turn next to the case that applied this question to minimum competency testing for the first time.

Notes

1. The first few notes in this chapter give some elementary background on certain aspects of the law in hopes of making the text a little clearer. These notes, however, do not pretend to be more than a very crude sketch of the law involved.

The minimum competency cases brought so far are *civil actions,* rather than criminal; those in the future will probably be civil also. The difference is important. In a civil action, one person or group sues another to be compensated for a wrong, or to have the wrong stopped or undone. There is no punishment as such, although the wrongdoer must pay for the damage he did if he loses. A criminal action, in contrast, is always brought by a government, usually seeking punishment in the form of fines or imprisonment. Television notwithstanding, the large preponderance of court business is civil, not criminal.

Formerly there were two distinct kinds of civil action, each heard in different courtrooms. In an action at *law,* the person suing could ask only for money to compensate him, with a few ancient and minor exceptions. In an action in *equity,* he could request that the court order someone else to do or not to do a certain thing. The two systems were merged in the federal courts in 1938, and today only a handful of states keep them separate. One difference still persists, however. Equity-type cases are always heard by a judge alone, never with a jury. Most minimum competency cases will probably be of this type and so will not involve juries.

2. A child under a certain age, usually 18 or 21, cannot sue on his own and requires an adult (in addition to the attorney) to appear for him in court. Often this adult is a parent, if one is living, though it need not be. It is the child, though, who receives the benefits from the suit.

3. Every state has a highest court and all the lower courts in that state must rule the same way as the highest court did on its most recent similar case. In the same way, the federal courts must follow the United States Courts of Appeal, of which there are 11, corresponding to 11 "circuits," or geographical areas of the country.

The U.S. Supreme Court, however, stands over both the state and federal systems. In federal matters, every court in the land must rule as the Supreme Court did most recently. The problem is, of course, that cases seldom have exactly similar facts. Attorneys will often argue that different earlier decisions should apply, or that earlier decisions should be interpreted differently. Until the Supreme Court rules squarely on a minimum competency dispute, there will always be some doubt as to the outcome of competency cases in lower courts, and plenty of room for lawyers to argue creatively.

4. 474 F. Supp. 244 (M.D. Fla. 1979). There are many more of these legal

citations in this chapter and the next. It is of no immediate consequence to the discussion, but for the interested, here is an explanation of the citation form.

The name of the case appears in the text, here *Debra P. v. Turlington.* The person suing, the plaintiff, is the first name in a trial decision such as this one; the person sued, the defendant, is the second name. The "v." of course is an abbreviation of "versus." In an appellate (appeals) decision, some jurisdictions name first the party who is appealing, though others keep the plaintiff first.

The *Debra P.* case actually had ten plaintiffs, all of them students represented in court by a parent or guardian, suing in a class action "on behalf of themselves and all other persons similarly situated." There were also fifteen individual defendants, all of them state or school officials, plus the state school department and the county board. Debra P. and Ralph Turlington happened to be the first named on each side. All other parties are omitted from the case name for brevity, though they do appear in the published opinion.

The first part of the citation simply tells where the published decision appears. "F. Supp." is an abbreviation of *"Federal Supplement,"* a series of books published by the West Publishing Company. *Federal Supplement* prints selected decisions of the lower federal courts and is available in most law libraries. The preceding number, here 474, is the volume number; the following number, 244, is the page on which the case report begins. In most such publications, the judge's opinion comes after a page or two of summary and indexing information. Last in the citation, in parentheses, is the court that handed down the decision—here, the federal District Court for the Middle District of Florida (M.D. Fla.) and the year of the decision.

Every legal citation follows a similar pattern, except that the abbreviation for the court will not appear if it can be inferred from the series of books in which the decision is published. For example, several other cases cited in this chapter are found in a series abbreviated "U.S." (see note 19). Since the U.S. series carries only Supreme Court decisions, a further indication of the court is unnecessary and only the date need appear in parentheses.

5. The loser in a lawsuit can appeal at least once, and sometimes more often. Here, both sides lost on different issues, and both sides are appealing. Because the case was first heard by a federal District Court—the trial courts for most cases in the federal system—the appeal goes to the United States Court of Appeals for the "circuit" in which the District Court was sitting, in this case the Fifth Circuit. Had the case been before a state trial court, the first appeal would have gone before a state appeals court.

The appeals court considers only the record from the trial court and the attorneys' arguments. It does not hear the case all over again. Both sides submit written briefs and usually present their views orally as well. The appealing attorney claims that the trial judge made legal errors, while his opponent argues that there were no errors. If the appeals court sees no error or finds the errors insignificant, it will let the trial judge's decision stand. Only rarely will an appeals court reopen the trial judge's version of the facts, that is, of what happened between the parties to bring on the lawsuit. The appeal most often concerns simply the application of law to whatever facts were established at trial.

6. 60 Cal. App. 3d 814, 131 Cal. Rptr. 854 (1976). There are two citations here because the same opinion was published in two different places.

7. *Id*. at 817, 131 Cal. Rptr. at 855.

8. *Id*. at 821, 131 Cal. Rptr. at 858.

9. On this point the court cites an earlier case, which in turn quotes from a much respected treatise on the subject: Prosser, *Law of Torts*.

10. 60 Cal. App. 3d at 824, 131 Cal. Rptr. at 860.

11. *Id*. at 825, 131 Cal. Rptr. at 861 (citations omitted).

12. At this writing, California plans to make graduation from high school conditional on passing a minimum competency test, effective with the 1980 graduating class (Pipho 1979*b*).

13. McClung, *Competency Testing Programs: Legal and Educational issues,* 47 Fordham L. Rev. 651, 661 n. 49 (1979). This paper is an objective, highly readable examination of many issues important to competency testing. Despite its appearance in a legal publication, nonlawyers should not hesitate to consult it. Most law libraries will have this journal on hand.

14. 418 N.Y.S.2d 375 (1979).

15. *Id*. at 377 (citations omitted).

16. McClung, *supra,* 47 Fordham L. Rev. at 661 n. 49, notes that the first appeal in *Donohue,* though not the second, did cite *Peter W.* with approval. McClung's article apparently went to press before the second appeal was decided. Readers doing research in the area might also note that a case McClung cites as awarding damages for educational malpractice, *Hoffman v. Board of Educ.,* 410 N.Y.S.2d 99 (1978), has since been reversed on a subsequent appeal, 424 N.Y.S.2d 376 (1979), thus bringing this case into line with *Peter W.* and *Donohue.* As the present book goes to press, there have not been any successful cases in educational malpractice.

17. 418 N.Y.S.2d at 378.

18. 474 F. Supp. 244 (M.D. Fla. 1979).

19. 347 U.S. 483 (1954).

20. *Id*. at 493.

21. *Id*. The famous phrase requiring desegregation "with all deliberate speed" occurs in a later opinion arising from the same case, *Brown v. Board of Educ.,* 349 U.S. 294, 301 (1955).

22. 426 U.S. 229 (1976).

23. *Id*. at 233.

24. *Id*. at 241.

25. *Id*. at 242 (citations omitted).

26. *Id*. at 235.

27. *Id*.

28. *Id*. at 253.

29. 429 U.S. 252 (1977).

30. *Id*. at 270.

31. 442 U.S. 256 (1979).

32. *Id*. at 271–272.

33. *Id*. at 272 (citations omitted).

34. *Id.* at 273.
35. *Id.* at 279 (citations omitted).
36. *Id.* at 279 n. 25.
37. *Id.* at 273.

7

The Case of Debra P.

T he first few cases in a new area of the law are often influential for many years afterward. The principles that such
cases establish typically become the law that other courts must
follow. A case does not achieve this status in a trial court,
however. Though other courts may look to the case for
guidance, a trial court's decision is not a precedent they must
follow. More far-reaching influence comes only after the case
has been heard on appeal. (See Note 5 in the preceding chapter
for a brief description of the appeals system.)

The decision on appeal has greater authority for three main
reasons. First, the decision may be different from that handed
down in the trial court. The appellate (appeals) court might let
the trial judge's ruling stand, modify it, or reverse it outright. It
is the appellate decision that constitutes the precedent from then
on. Second, the ruling on appeal is legally binding on all of the
lower courts coming under that appellate court. A trial judge
must follow such rulings made by the courts over him or he too
will be reversed on appeal. And when an issue in federal law
reaches the U.S. Supreme Court, the highest appellate court of
all, the opinion is binding on every other court in the United
States. (Washington lawyers insist there is a higher court
still—the basketball court on the top floor of the Supreme
Court building, where the justices' clerks discuss how best to influence the members of the Court downstairs.) Finally, the appellate court typically pays more attention to the principles of
law and less to the facts of the particular case than does the trial
court below. For that reason, its holding may apply to a broader
range of cases in the future.

The case we shall look at here has not yet been decided on appeal. That is important, because it severely limits the applicability of the opinion to other situations and other jurisdictions. But the case is worth careful attention nonetheless. It is the only minimum competency case that has been ruled on so far; thus other courts are paying close attention to it, though they are not legally obliged to do so. And more important, the case demonstrates how a judge can take a new set of facts, test them against the legal precedents he must follow, and arrive at a decision. This can be a difficult task, when the precedents do not anticipate the particular situation that the judge must decide.

This case is interesting for another reason: The precedents might have justified an outcome that would have been unjust. (The losing side, of course, is always likely to consider the outcome unjust.) In this case, the court reached a conclusion that both sides should be able to live with — not always easy to do — though both sides have appealed it. The appeals, in this instance, may be more to obtain an authoritative statement on the law than to obtain relief from the trial judge's decision.

In reaching its decision, the court necessarily had to approve some legal theories in the case and strike down others as invalid. The opinion thus includes, between the lines, a set of instructions on how to prepare similar lawsuits in the future. Attorneys are reading it carefully. As a result, the second wave of suits are likely to be better focused and more sharply reasoned. This initial case can influence the conduct of other suits, and hence possibly their outcomes, for many years in the future.

The case is *Debra P. v. Turlington.*[1] Its facts are simple enough. In 1976, Florida enacted minimum competency legislation; in 1978, the state legislature amended the law to require that students pass the test in order to receive high school diplomas. Students who expected to graduate in 1979 thus learned on very short notice that the rules of the game had changed. In addition to fulfilling their other requirements, they now also had to pass a test known as SSAT II in order to graduate.

The state's experience with the test had been brief, as instructional objectives for the test were not sent to the schools until the summer of 1977; but it was sufficient to reveal a major problem. Black students, as a group, were not doing very well in the preliminary trials, though white students performed adequately. The court's calculation, adjusting the raw figures for the smaller number of blacks in the school population, showed that about 20 percent of black students could not pass in three attempts, but only 1.9 percent of whites failed all three times.[2] In other words, a substantial number of black students would be leaving school without diplomas, once the new law went into effect. The number of whites affected would be very small; in social terms almost negligible.

Black twelfth graders viewed the situation with understandable alarm. The requirement seemed on its face to be discriminatory, as black students' chances of success were considerably worse than those of their white counterparts. Accordingly, a number of students brought suit, seeking to enjoin the state from denying diplomas on the basis of the test.

Their suit took the form of a class action. In practical terms, this meant that a decision in court would be binding not only on the people who actually sued, but also on all others whom they described in their class. The court must "certify" a class, by finding that its members have enough interests in common for a decision affecting them all as a group to be reasonable. A court will certify only if the class is too numerous for all of its members to take part in the case themselves, among other requirements. But once the class is certified (and it was, in this case), then the outcome of the case applies to everyone described in it.

There were actually three classes certified in *Debra P.* The first consisted of "all present and future twelfth grade public school students in the State of Florida who have failed or who hereafter fail the SSAT II."[3] Parenthetically, this meant that an injunction against the test, in favor of this class, would affect the test's use for all graduating students in Florida, whether or not they appeared in court and including even those who never heard of the suit. The other two classes were smaller. The second class consisted only of black students who fit the description above, and the third was further restricted to black students in a particular Florida county.

The three classes brought specific complaints, as one always must in filing a lawsuit. Except as noted, all three classes made the following three claims:

1. That the new test is biased, and that it violates the equal protection clause of the fourteenth amendment and various statutes;

2. That the very short notice of the new requirement also violates the fourteenth amendment; and

3. (Black students only) that the testing program was resegregating the schools by sending mostly black students to remediation classes.

The court ruled favorably on the first two of these claims and rejected the third. It enjoined use of the test to withhold students' diplomas for a period of four years.

The first claim, the discrimination issue, is perhaps the most interesting because it is the most likely to recur in subsequent cases. The question of notice is easier for the states to avoid, simply by having long enough phase-in periods. And resegregation in remedial classrooms may be a dead issue, after this case. But charges of discrimination are likely to persist as long as more blacks than whites fail the tests.

The diploma sanction is too important to ignore. As the court put it, "The denial of a standard diploma based on the failure of the SSAT II triggers a number of economic and academic deprivations."[4] Elsewhere the court also referred to psychological harm.[5] Although Judge Carr expressed optimism in the *Debra P.* opinion that racial differences in test results will even out over the next few years, that hope may turn out to be unrealistic. The courts may be busy for a far longer time than that.

The plaintiffs approached their claim of discrimination from several directions. For reasons we shall examine below, the court chose to focus on one of them: "The essence of the [discrimination] claim is the Plaintiffs' contention that SSAT II perpetuates and reemphasizes the effects of past purposeful discrimination."[6] The complaint charged further, and more specifically, that the test bore no correlation to the curriculum, that it was racially biased, and that the high failure rate among black students was a foreseeable consequence of implementing the test.

In order for the court to find discrimination, the facts would have to meet the conditions laid out in three Supreme Court cases we have already discussed, here expressed in terms of the testing situation: *Washington v. Davis*[7] (intent to discriminate), *Arlington Heights* (suspicious procedures in setting up the test requirement), and *Feeney* (requiring the test because of, not just in spite of, the resulting discriminating impact). All three cases, moreover, require that the state have a "legitimate interest" in making success on the test a requirement for graduation.

The judge's task in *Debra P.* was complicated by an accident of legal chronology. The Supreme Court decided the *Feeney* case after the *Debra P.* trial was over but before the decision was handed down. Ordinarily the attorneys for both sides argue how prior cases apply, and ordinarily a court is reluctant to rule without hearing such arguments in full.[8] In this case, however, the court had to work through the *Feeney* analysis without the benefit of counsels' reasoning for their respective sides.

Before taking up *Feeney,* the court made a simple, two-step argument to establish discriminatory intent. First, from *Washington v. Davis,* "[T]he actor is presumed to have intended the natural consequences of his deeds."[9] And second,

[I]t is clear that the most significant official decision maker, the Commissioner of Education, Ralph Turlington, foresaw that the effect of the implementation of the SSAT II would result in greatly disproportionate numbers of black failures. Even in the face of actual statistics regarding the number of black failures on the field tests and the early administrations, the Commissioner persisted in his opinion that the diploma sanction should be implemented in the 1978–1979 school term.[10]

In short, black failure was a natural consequence of the test and, according to *Washington v. Davis,* was therefore intended. One requirement for intent was established.

Before *Feeney,* this might have been enough to find discrimination. But the appearance of *Feeney* upset this easy analysis. After *Feeney,* a proof of intent had to show that the test was implemented because of, not merely in spite of, its discriminatory impact. There was no such proof in this case—and for excellent reason. Neither the attorneys nor the judge could know that such evidence might be material, for the "because of" language became law only after the trial was over. Yet without the evidence, under the *Feeney* opinion the court could not find intent to discriminate. And without intent, the court could not find unconstitutional discrimination under *Washington v. Davis.*

It was a troubling situation. The court had to find discrimination if it was to give the black students in Florida any relief. And some kind of relief was plainly needed, in light of the statistics on black failure; otherwise the court would be concluding by implication that black students were inherently inferior academically. The problem was to circumvent the intent requirement, and Judge Carr rose to the occasion:

> [T]he Court has not been presented with sufficient proof that the motivation for implementing the [testing] program was in *Feeney* terms "because of" the large black failure statistics. . . . Although the proof of present intent to discriminate is insufficient, the Court is of the opinion that *past purposeful discrimination* affecting [the black] Plaintiffs . . . is perpetuated by the test and the diploma sanction regardless of its neutrality.[11]

Thus the decision rested not on the test itself, nor on the intent of the people giving the test, but on educational conditions that prevailed in Florida long before anyone had heard of minimum competency testing and diploma sanctions.

To support its holding that the test perpetuates past discrimination, the court pointed to Florida educational history. In at least some parts of the state, the schools had remained segregated until 1971, in apparent violation of *Brown v. Board of Education.*[12] The black plaintiffs in *Debra P.* started school in 1967 and so spent their first four years in all-black schools.

Under *Brown,* that alone gave them an inferior education, for legal purposes, during those first four years. The court determined that their education was inferior not only in the legal sense but in actuality as well:

[T]he Plaintiffs produced vast amounts of evidence of the inferiority in fact of black schools during the period 1967–1971. The evidence clearly indicates that black public schools in Florida were inferior in their physical facilities, course offerings, instructional materials, and equipment. There is little doubt but that the pervasive racial isolation condemned in *Brown* in conjunction with the inferiority of black schools created an atmosphere which was not as conducive to learning as that found in white schools. Further, this educational environment constituted a serious impairment to [black] Plaintiffs' ability to learn, especially in the early grades which most educators view as a formative stage in intellectual development.[13]

Moreover, and key to its decision, the court found that educational discrimination against black children did not end with the close of segregation:

Black children in the period after segregation ended were presented with numerous problems. Not only did the [black] Plaintiffs have to adjust to social, cultural and linguistic differences of the integrated schools, but they had to do so without an adequate educational foundation. The vestiges of the inferior elementary education they received still are present and affect their performance. Although remediation is now underway in a meaningful sense, the effects of past purposeful segregation have not been erased or overcome.[14]

The case against the test, in short, is that it penalizes black children now for the inferior education provided them in the past. The discriminatory intent is not in the people giving the test, but in those who kept the schools segregated between 1967 and 1971. Though not faulty in itself, the test is still not permissible because it gives present effect to the discrimination of the past.

There were two other ways in which the court might have

found discrimination without *Feeney* intent, but the evidence did not bear out either of them. First, there might have been racial bias in the test items themselves, as the plaintiffs charged. The court considered both the test review process and a mathematical analysis that looked for bias in the results and concluded,

> While some of the questions do seem to have factual settings un-familiar to certain racial groups, the Court is of the opinion that this distraction is minimal and unpervasive. The Court is not convinced by the Plaintiffs' evidence that the test or any item should be invalidated for racial or ethnic bias.[15]

Second, the test could have been struck down if it was not a reasonable component of the state's overall educational respon-sibilities. That is, if the test served no purpose useful to the state, its discriminatory impact would be unconstitutional whether intended or not. There does not seem to have been much dispute on this point.

> The legitimate interest in implementing a test to evaluate the established state-wide objectives is obvious. The minimal objec-tives established could be continually upgraded and the test could be utilized not only to gauge achievement, but also to identify deficiencies for the purpose of remediation.[16]

The court could not have decided the case without placing the blame somewhere, but its choices were limited in that respect. Having found that the test itself was not significantly biased, the court basically had only the following possibilities to consider: unequal intelligence, unequal environments, or unequal school-ing. That is, unless it ruled against the school system, the court would be letting stand the proposition that black students are indeed less capable than whites, because of inferior genes or en-vironment.

It would have been an awkward conclusion, even if it satisfied the legal precedents. Any hint of genetic inferiority would have run against the great weight of current authority in psychology, not to mention common sense. Nor did the opinion mention environmental factors at all. Ordinarily a court will not introduce a theory of its own; it relies on the parties to bring it the raw materials for a decision. Perhaps neither party wanted to make environmental considerations an issue, as such considerations might have worked against either side.

As it happened, however, the court was spared the necessity of what it called "punishing the victims." And it was able to reach its decision without criticizing current educational practices in Florida, except for the diploma sanction. The blame fell entirely on history, on unequal schooling in the past. That, said the court, is why black students are doing poorly on the test today, and that is what makes the diploma sanction unconstitutional.

> In the Court's opinion, punishing the victims of past discrimination for deficits created by an inferior educational environment neither constitutes a remedy nor creates better educational opportunities. . . . The Court must conclude that utilization of the SSAT II in the present context as a requirement for the receipt of a high school diploma is a violation of the equal protection clause of the Fourteenth Amendment [and two federal statutes].[17]

Accordingly, the court enjoined the state from using the test as a diploma requirement for four years, until the school year 1982–1983. By then, students in twelfth grade will have spent all of their Florida education in desegregated schools.

In the last passage quoted above, I omitted an important sentence so as to give it a separate discussion here: "When students regardless of race are permitted to commence and pursue their education in a unitary school system without the taint of the dual school system, then a graduation requirement based on a neutral test will be permitted."[18] This remark is wholly consistent with the finding that the high failure rate among blacks is due to segregated schooling during their first four years. But it raises two questions. Does it mean that states that have been legally desegregated for twelve years can now make a competency test a diploma requirement, even if many more blacks than whites are failing? And second, what are the implications

for Florida if—as may be the case—there is still a racial difference in the results four years after the *Debra P.* decision?

Merle McClung (1979) offers an answer to the first question,
urging caution even among states that have long been
desegregated:

> One serious misreading of the *Debra P.* decision by some states
> is that its legal rationale applies only to Southern states with a
> history of *de jure* segregation. This is a questionable interpreta-
> tion. . . . [T]he discrimination holding was based on the con-
> stitutional prohibition against programs that carry forward the
> effects of prior discrimination. The fact of earlier court findings
> of *de jure* segregation in Florida schools made it logical for the
> *Debra P.* court to cite this history as proof of prior discrimina-
> tion, but the legal principle would also encompass other
> evidence or findings of prior racial discrimination.

Presumably many other school systems, even where segregation
has not been tolerated by the courts for decades, would still be
susceptible to charges of recent discrimination in fact. Even in
Florida, a court might find residual effects of segregation per-
sisting after 1983. McClung also stresses the *Debra P.* finding of
inadequate notice of the new requirement (which we take up
below); this part of the decision applies to all Florida students
regardless of race, and regardless of when racial segregation
ceased.

The other question, that of racial differences that may remain
after four years, is more troublesome. For the sake of argument, let us suppose that four years later the differences have
diminished, due to remediation and the passage of time after
desegregation. But some differences remain, let us say. As long
as a substantially higher proportion of blacks than whites are
denied diplomas, further litigation is inevitable. How might a
Florida court rule after 1983, in light of *Debra P.*?

One possibility is a strict adherence to the *Debra P.* formula.
That would make the test and diploma sanction constitutional,
on the presumption that enough years have elapsed since
desegregation to give all students an equal opportunity to pass.
Such an outcome is unlikely, however, because it leads back to
the untenable implication that blacks are less capable of learn-

ing than whites. Or, a court might find that the test itself is racially biased after all.

It seems more probable, though, that a court would look for evidence of other, more subtle vestiges of past discrimination that have been carried into the present. Indeed, it would be a simple exercise in logic to conclude that the differences in test results prove there has been effective discrimination. Nor is that a circular argument, given the starting point that the races are inherently equal in potential.

A holding along those lines would put the schools in a difficult situation. As long as racial differences prevailed, they would be unable to impose the diploma sanction against any students, black or white. That would bring considerable pressure to bear on the schools—to find out why black students are not doing as well as whites and to correct the situation. Such an effort could be undertaken at any time, of course, without waiting for a court injunction. But so far, few educators have devoted themselves wholeheartedly to the problem. One of the few real benefits that could accrue from minimum competency testing—one that the states will fight hard to avoid—would be a legal obligation to make education in fact equal for all.

Other Issues in *Debra P.*

There is more in the *Debra P.* opinion, but most of it need not detain us long. Alongside the discrimination issue, the court gave equal weight to the fact that students and teachers alike had very little warning of the test as a diploma requirement. This lack of notice was a second reason for the court's enjoining the withholding of diplomas for four years.

> The Plaintiffs, after spending ten years in schools where their attendance was compelled, were informed of a requirement concerning skills which, if taught, should have been taught in grades they had long since completed. While it is impossible to determine if all the skills were taught to all the students, it is obvious that the instruction given was not presented in an educational atmosphere directed by the existence of specific objectives and stimulated throughout the period of instruction by a diploma sanction. These are the two ingredients which the Defendants

[i.e., the state] assert are essential to the program at the present time. The Court is of the opinion that the inadequacy of the notice provided prior to the invocation of the diploma sanction, the objectives, and the test is a violation of the due process clause [of the fourteenth amendment].[19]

Lurking in that passage is a phrase that may provide yet another argument for extending an injunction against the diploma sanction, if indeed racial differences persist after the injunction period. That is the idea that certain skills are best taught in certain grades. Elsewhere the court made this thought more explicit: "The evidence indicates that the instruction of functional literacy skills to older students is more difficult, particularly because the unidentified deficiencies of earlier years have become ingrained."[20] This reasoning might enable a court, if it wishes, to postpone the diploma sanction for a full ten or twelve years after a minimum competency program was announced, that is, until graduating students will have spent their early years in a competency environment. With the principle of adequate notice now established in *Debra P.,* there may be room for considerable flexibility in determining just how much notice is enough.

The school system argued in *Debra P.* that it needed to apply the diploma sanction immediately to put pressure on students to pass the test. That, it felt, would encourage students to learn their basic skills. The court acknowledged that the sanction might have that beneficial effect. But it considered the question of adequate notice to be far more important, as shown by the strong language it chose to sum up that part of the opinion:

> While the denial of the diploma has a certain deterrent value, its application in the instant case would be analagous to asserting that the immediate and indefinite incarceration without a trial of an individual upon the suspicion of the commission of a crime would have a deterrent effect on other potential offenders. No doubt it would. But in our country, the Constitution, including the due process clause, stands between the arbitrary government action and the innocent individual.[21]

A third issue in the case, along with discrimination and inadequate notice, was the question of whether students had in fact been taught the skills being tested. If they had not, then it would be patently unfair to deny them diplomas for failing, as the failure could hardly be attributed to any shortcoming on the students' part. Merle McClung (1977) goes farther: A test that withholds diplomas on the basis of skills not taught may be so arbitrary as to violate due process of law.

McClung has identified two conditions that a test should meet to conform with due process in this respect; he terms them *curricular validity* and *instructional validity*. To have curricular validity, a test can examine only those skills listed in the state's published curriculum. Otherwise, students and teachers will not be on notice that the skill may be required for a diploma. For example, if finding information in the Yellow Pages were not among a state's professed educational objectives, then a minimum competency item requiring that skill would presumably lack curricular validity.

The mere listing of an objective does not ensure that a student will actually be exposed to it in the classroom, however. Indeed, prior to competency testing, it was common for teachers to overlook published objectives if they thought other topics more important. Accordingly, instructional validity is the condition that a test examine only skills that were covered in actual instruction. Without instructional validity, a test does not belong in the schools at all.

The *Debra P.* court examined only curricular validity, and not even that to the plaintiffs' satisfaction. The court seems, in fact, to have invoked curricular validity to counter the students' claim that the test lacked content validity, which is quite a different thing. In this context, a test with content validity is one that actually examines whatever subject matter (content) it purports to examine. For example, something sold as a math test which in fact measured mostly reading skills would be very low in content validity.

The validity dispute in *Debra P.* was largely a matter of labeling. The Florida legislature had spoken in terms of "functional literacy," and the test in its early versions was called a test of functional literacy. (The name was later changed to SSAT II, the State Student Assessment Test II, in a futile attempt to improve the test's public image.) The plaintiffs argued that the test should live up to its name and in fact ought to test functional literacy—especially considering that students who failed it would carry the label of functional illiterates. Yet the evidence showed at least 11 known definitions of functional literacy. Presumably no one test can satisfy all of them. Moreover, said the plaintiffs, the test does not match any of the definitions, and so it lacks content validity.

The court was not impressed with this line of argument. The real question, it said, was merely whether the test provided a reasonable basis for determining who would receive diplomas and who would not. And since the state unquestionably had the power to set educational goals, the issue came down to whether the test conformed to those goals.

> [T]he Court in this case can only be concerned with whether the test reasonably or arbitrarily evaluates the skill objectives established by the State Board of Education. Thus, the Court must not focus on the title of the test or the public perceptions of functional literacy, but rather must analyze the test from the perspective of its objectives and the definition provided by its designers.[22]

The first sentence of this quotation contains a reasonable definition of curricular validity. And in the second sentence, the court seems to assert that it will not consider content validity at all, as long as the condition of curricular validity is satisfied.

Curricular validity, however, is a relatively easy condition to meet. Almost anyone can take a list of objectives and design a test around them, especially in states that express their objectives in behavioral terms. Consider, for example, these objectives from the Florida list, one from each of the two required categories. In communications: "The student will, in a real world situation, distinguish between facts and opinions." And in mathematics: "The student will determine the solution to real world problems involving purchases and a rate of sales tax."[23]

As a rule, it is not difficult to construct test items that reflect such objectives faithfully. The items may be faulty for other reasons, but that is not the issue here. And once the items are a reasonable match to the objectives, then the court's requirements for curricular validity are apparently satisfied. As the court seemingly equated content validity with curricular validity, content validity would thus also be satisfied.

Other courts may follow *Debra P.* in this respect; if they do not, they may have to rule on a tangle of expert opinions about validity instead. (Recall those 11 definitions of functional literacy.) Yet if *Debra P.* becomes the rule, then neither content nor curricular validity will be much of an issue in most future litigation. The states should have little trouble in establishing both, simply by introducing their published objectives alongside the test.

According to McClung (1977), however, curricular validity is not enough. The test must have instructional validity as well, i.e., must examine only material that was actually taught. This was an issue that the *Debra P.* court sidestepped altogether: "[I]t is impossible to determine if all the skills were taught to all the students."[24] Indeed, it mattered little in this particular case whether the students had received appropriate instruction or not because the findings of discrimination and inadequate notice were enough to justify the injunction against the test.

In other cases, however, instructional validity may become much more of an issue, particularly for plaintiffs who cannot prove there was discrimination or an inadequate notice period. Instructional validity ought to make a good argument. A state will find it hard to defend a diploma denial when the state itself did not provide the instruction that students would have needed to pass the test.

Even a state that is in the right, moreover, may find it extremely difficult to establish instructional validity. In Judge Carr's words, the point may remain "impossible to determine." A proof of instructional validity might require establishing in the courtroom that every student tested had sufficient instruction in all of the needed skills. There will be disagreement on how much instruction is enough. In view of the *Debra P.* finding that some skills are best taught early, the year in which the instruction was given might become a factor. But that could require defendant state educational systems to track down records of particular students from ten years earlier. What of students who move into the state during the course of their education? The situation promotes the unlikely fantasy of states getting together to establish a uniform national curriculum, simply to validate their individual competency tests.

By avoiding the question, the *Debra P.* court left the future of instructional validity uncertain. When instructional validity does come up for a ruling, there will be two competing positions. A diploma denial resulting from the student's failure to learn material that was never taught would be fundamentally unjust. It would violate the most basic ideas of fair play in American law. But school systems will point to the practical difficulties of proving that every student had enough classroom exposure to every topic. Depending on the thoroughness of proof required, proof may be all but impossible. The consequence, the schools will say, will be to strike down competency testing for all students and to forego the hoped for improvements in education, on the off chance that one or two students here and there may have missed a topic.

As a practical matter, the outcome may turn on who carries the burden of proof as to instructional validity. Must the students prove instructional validity is lacking, or must the schools prove it is established? *Debra P.* gives us no indication. The burden of proof is especially important when proof is difficult, because then the party with the burden is likely to lose the case.

Remediation

One last point in this case deserves attention. One of the plaintiffs' major claims, in addition to discrimination, inadequate notice, and invalidity of the test, focused on remediation. A companion statute to the state's competency legislation requires Florida schools to provide remediation for students who fail the test. But as the failing students are disproportionately black, so are the remediation classes. The plaintiffs maintained that the testing program resegregated Florida classrooms, in violation of the fourteenth amendment and certain federal statutes.

This claim was unsuccessful, even though the court

acknowledged that resegregation of certain classrooms was a result of the procedure. The court took into account the fact that student composition in the remedial program changed constantly as people moved in and out. No fixed population was involved. The program occupied at most two hours a day. Most important, the court observed that the program aimed to reduce black failure in the competency test and with promising results. "By the end of the Court's [four year] injunction, all students should be ready and able to compete on an equal footing."[25] In terms of the rest of the opinion, this might imply that segregated remediation classes will cease to be legally acceptable once the entire school population has had its whole education in desegregated schools. Or, perhaps it merely expresses the court's optimism that the injunction will have its intended effect.

The court also had a warning for the schools: "The defendants must be constantly wary that the utilization of the SSAT I and II and the compensatory education program do not isolate and stigmatize any children for longer than is necessary to compensate for the identified deficits."[26]

Summary of the *Debra P.* Opinion

There is a great deal of material in the *Debra P.* opinion, not all of which we have looked at here. There are also many issues the opinion does not raise, and which may come up in the future. But before we come to those, a brief summary of *Debra P.* may be helpful.

The court found the diploma sanction unconstitutional in two respects: it carried forward the effects of past purposeful discrimination—i.e., past segregation in Florida—and it gave students and teachers insufficient notice. But the court found nothing wrong with the test itself. On the contrary, the opinion notes that the test was free of significant ethnic or racial bias, and that it satisfied requirements as to curricular and content validity. There was no finding, one way or the other, on the important question of instructional validity. Nor did the court enjoin use of the test itself—only its application as a graduation requirement. The state was even allowed to retain scores from the test, "in a fashion consistent with the manner in which the state retains other achievement test scores."[27]

The state has appealed the four-year injunction. The plaintiffs also have appealed on several points: that the injunction is not long enough to prevent discrimination; that the test is racially and ethnically biased and does not have instructional validity; and that the test is educationally unjustified.

(Just as this chapter was completed, Judge Carr handed down a second decision. His first injunction had named the SSAT specifically. So two Florida counties tried to circumvent the injunction by using their own test, not the SSAT. The *Debra P.* students complained that this was an attempt to "thwart, frustrate, defeat, cripple, undermine, defy and hinder" the ruling they had won. Judge Carr agreed, issuing a new preliminary injunction to bar the counties from "using any scheme or artifice or testing procedure" as a requirement for high school graduation. That, too, is now on its way to an appeal. [*Education Daily,* May 27, 1980].)

States that do not use competency scores to withhold diplomas need not expect any problems to arise from the *Debra P.* decision. And states that provide several years for phasing in the diploma sanction should be able to withstand challenge on the notice issue. The major application of this case is likely to be on the question of discrimination.

Other Issues for the Future

It is also possible, even likely, that future lawsuits will raise arguments not ruled on in *Debra P.* Instructional validity may be one. And some of the other criticisms of minimum competency testing raised earlier in this book may offer viable arguments in court.

There has been much litigation recently on the rights of handicapped students. In every case decided to date, the courts have required the schools to provide whatever compensation the handicap may require. The goal is an education that resembles as closely as possible that afforded to nonhandicapped children (Lazarus 1980*b*). In particular, the courts have been very alert to any sign of discrimination against handicapped students. It seems unlikely that the courts will approve the denial of a diploma to a handicapped student if there is any possibility that either the test results, or the education leading up to the test, were in any way impeded by the handicap. The Office for Civil Rights has warned that it may be a violation of federal law to withhold diplomas from handicapped students on the basis of a minimum competency test.

There may also be suits brought on behalf of gifted children. Under the pressure of competency legislation, some states are reallocating funds for teaching very basic skills and for remediation for students having trouble with those skills. This change can work to the disadvantage of students who are performing well above the minimum level. Amidst all the rhetoric of tailoring education to each child's individual needs, gifted children might argue that competency testing harms them. To their detriment, competency testing establishes a favored class of students, those who are operating near the competency borderline.

Moreover, there is an argument still to be raised in court that the technology of testing is not sufficiently advanced to meet the demands of competency programs. Any test result is in error, to a certain extent. And any decision based on test scores will result in a certain number of students wrongly judged. It is even possible to compute with some accuracy just how many students will be so affected, though not to identify them by name.

A case based on this argument will be interesting. A student who failed a competency test will prove in court, with reasonable certainty, that the chances are one in four that he should have passed — or one chance in twenty, or one in a hundred. How certain must it be that a student's failure to pass the test was due to a lack of skills, rather than chance error, in order to justify withholding a diploma? Courts usually prefer not to play with numerical probabilities. But if the court picks any probability at all, it will effectively strike down the diploma sanction altogether. Suppose the court specifies that a student's failure to pass must be 99 percent certain to have resulted from a lack of skills. The school system must then lower its cutoff score until a student who falls below the new score will be 99 percent certain to have truly failed at the old score. But then another student who comes under the new, lower score can raise just the same test-error argument. The process of lowering cutoff scores can repeat itself endlessly, one step down per lawsuit, until the cutoff vanishes altogether.

As yet, there have been no suits based on the language question, where a student is literate in his own tongue but fails a test in English. A student who moves into a minimum competency state in the closing years of his education might argue that the diploma sanction should not apply to him — the notice question again, in different guise. No doubt there will also be arguments on religious grounds, paralleling the many cases on compulsory attendance laws (Lazarus 1980a); someone is certain to argue that the minimum competency laws violate religious freedoms. A student who has been suspended for disciplinary reasons, and therefore barred from instruction, might argue that the state by its own actions contributed to his failure and therefore should not apply the diploma sanction against him.

Not all such suits will necessarily prevail, but they all give rise to interesting legal arguments. *Debra P.* is only a start in resolving the disputes over minimum competency. Even that case is not over, as both sides have appealed. Other cases will certainly be brought in the meantime, before *Debra P.* is finally disposed of. Even with Judge Carr's opinion in *Debra P.* before us, it is much too early to know how those later cases will fare.

Notes

1. 474 F. Supp. 244 (M.D. Fla. 1979).
2. *Id.* at 253.
3. *Id.* at 246.
4. *Id.* at 249.
5. *Id.* at 266.
6. *Id.* at 250.
7. See Chapter 6 for the citations to this case and the two following.
8. This general rule has famous exceptions. Some of the landmark cases in American law have resulted from the judges ruling on points that had not even occurred to the attorneys.
9. 426 U.S. at 253.
10. 474 F. Supp. at 254.
11. *Id.* at 254–255 (emphasis added).
12. See note 19 in the preceding chapter and accompanying text.

13. 474 F. Supp. at 251–252 (footnotes omitted).
14. *Id.* at 252.
15. *Id.* at 261–262.
16. *Id.* at 254.
17. *Id.* at 257.
18. *Id.*
19. *Id.* at 267.
20. *Id.*
21. *Id.* (citations omitted).
22. *Id.* at 260.
23. *Id.* at 259 n. 22.
24. *Id.* at 267.
25. *Id.* at 268.
26. *Id.*
27. *Id.* at 269.

8

Goodbye to Excellence

I n the end, whether minimum competency testing makes sense or not comes to depend on what we think is the purpose of education. If education is *only* to fit the student for daily life, by equipping him with certain basic skills, then competency testing is a step in the right direction. A test puts pressure on teachers and students to make sure the tested skills are mastered, especially when diploma sanction is involved. The same test identifies students along the way who are behind schedule in acquiring the skills. It helps channel funding for instruction in these skills and encourages remediation to help children who may be in danger of not learning them at all. For the public, and particularly for employers, the test distinguishes people leaving school who have the skills from those who do not.

By its nature, competency testing serves the lowest common denominator of education, the irreducible core. Of course it does, say its advocates; that is why we call it "minimum competency." The intent is merely to make sure that all students gain at least a certain amount of education. In theory, there is nothing to stop students and teachers from ascending as far above the minimum as their interests and abilities can take them. Unfortunately, however, it does not seem to be working out that way in practice.

As in economics, there is a kind of Gresham's Law in education. The economic version has it that "bad money drives out good." When clad-copper coins were introduced in the United States to replace silver coins, the silver coins all but disappeared overnight. If metal worth a couple of pennies could pass for twenty-five cents, why spend the same weight in valuable silver instead? A silver quarter today will bring many times its face value from a coin dealer. But in circulation — handed to a bus driver — it is still worth only twenty-five cents. With the appearance of cheap money, in other words, expensive money promptly went elsewhere.

A diploma is currency, of a kind. Physically it is a piece of paper with writing on it, practically worthless in itself, like a dollar bill. But the diploma, like the dollar, stands for something far more valuable. Its worth is measured by the strength it represents, by the promise that stands behind it. The United States promises to honor its dollars by accepting them in payment of debts. Thus the taxpayer need not lug his gold down to the Internal Revenue Service; the government will take his paper money instead. In the same sort of way, the school promises to honor its diploma, by making available for the common good a person with the education that the diploma represents. That is the strength, the promise, that turns the diploma from a mere sheet of foolscap into a document of value.

Looking at the diploma as currency, what effect does minimum competency have on its worth — on its purchasing power, so to speak? Advocates would argue — have argued, in fact — that minimum competency makes the diploma more valuable. Before the competency programs (according to this view), diplomas were essentially worthless. Illiterates carried them, people with no hope of redeeming the promise implied on the face of the document. That makes for a weak currency. But with the competency programs in effect, every diploma is assured at least a certain minimum value in terms of its holder's capabilities.

That much is true. But the argument overlooks a significant fact: both before and during minimum competency testing, the large majority of people with diplomas have *not* been illiterate. Most perform well above the minimum levels. There are only a few percent, after all, who fail the competency tests; the rest have always been able to prove at least the minimum. And since most students cluster near the middle in ability, in something like a bell-shaped curve, the bulk of the group should always sit well above the cutoff level.

The problem with giving value to diplomas is that they all take on the same value, regardless of each student's true worth. Before minimum competency testing, when anyone could have a diploma simply by sitting in school long enough, a diploma had no value at all for practical purposes. But there were still good students and bad students, and people who wanted to know which was which were able to find out. Competency diplomas make a single partition in the group, one of limited usefulness—between very poor students and everybody else.

The "everybody else" is where Gresham's Law takes hold, in one of its educational versions. The minimum competency diploma has little value. It promises very limited capabilities. But once in circulation, as it were, it is likely to drive out other, more informative credentials such as transcripts and employers' own evaluations. There are still good and bad students among those who pass, but a single-valued diploma tends to mask the differences among them. Unless the diploma were meaningful to some degree, it could not have that effect; a shapeless lump of copper has no value as money. Only when shaped into a quarter does it push out the more valuable silver coin. Diplomas too, once given a fixed, minimal significance, have the power to drive out credentials of greater intrinsic worth and to place the same low value on all graduating students.

What is worse, Gresham's Law operates back at the mint, too: Once the first copper coin is struck, there can be no more silver ones. It would be foolish after that to melt down more silver for coins, when copper will now make a coinage worth just as much in circulation. Over the years, the schools may come to a parallel conclusion—that it makes little sense to strive for excellence, when achieving it gives the diploma no greater value in circulation. To a problem-plagued, debt-ridden school system, the temptation will become very strong to bring students up to the diploma requirements and not much farther.

Let me come to this point another way, because it is important. In the competency view, one goal of education is to equip the student with at least certain minimum skills. The diploma is his mark of having acquired those skills. Such is an educator's picture of the situation. But the student is likely to see it otherwise, considering the priorities that society urges on young people nowadays. Why, after all, do people go to high school? No doubt a few are there simply because they love to learn. But many more are in school because their parents insist that they graduate, or because they need the diploma for college or for a job.

The student's perspective is thus likely to run opposite to the educator's view that the skills constitute the goal. To the student, the goal is most often to acquire a diploma. Learning the skills is just something he must do to meet that goal, very much a secondary concern. In the end it is the diploma that people will ask to see, not the skills — once they are assured that the diploma is "meaningful."

This is simply a case of confusing the credential with the qualifications for it, not an uncommon turn of events in our credential-conscious society. It is especially likely to arise when requirements for the credential purport to establish a minimum level of ability. For example, in states where car mechanics need not be licensed, we ask around carefully before choosing one to repair our car. Yet some of us are more likely to trust a physician or an attorney whom we know less about, simply because he has the right papers on the office wall — and without them, we know, he would not have an office at all. The credential comes to substitute for the qualifications.

That is precisely the purpose of awarding credentials, of course — to help people determine others' qualifications without a lot of detailed investigation. In a competency state, a high school diploma is supposed to serve much the same purpose for employers. But in consequence, the actual qualifications become far less important. It is the diploma that matters, regardless of what it represents.

Mechanisms for awarding credentials, including competency tests, are necessarily insensitive to people's individual strengths and weaknesses. The price of convenience in ascertaining someone's qualifications, by way of a credential, is almost total ignorance of those same qualifications. There is no contradiction involved. One can ask for a little information, or a lot. The minimum competency diploma is handy for employers precisely because it tells them very little — just that this student passed the test. More information—a transcript, for example, or teachers' observations about the student—would only detract from the convenience of having to consider just a single piece of paper.

A credential, in short, compresses a great deal of information about a person into a single yes or no answer. Indeed, information theory tells us that this is the least amount of information that any message can carry.[1] And to arrive at that one particle of information, educators must overlook nearly everything they know about their students.

Letter grades carry more information, but not much. The problem of compressing information remains. I learned this in the trenches—mine was a particularly comfortable trench—in my first evaluation of students. As a graduate teaching assistant in electrical engineering labs, I shepherded my little flock of sophomores through the mysteries of elementary circuit analysis. Working with the same dozen or so students twice a week, I came to know most of them quite well. Too well, in fact, to assign a letter grade that properly summarized their accomplishments. They simply refused to fit neatly into As, Bs, and Cs. But two years later, I had the much easier task in an elementary psychology course of grading five hundred students at a stroke. That was just a matter of adding up quiz scores and plotting a curve. Knowing practically nothing about the students, I was able to grade them with confidence. The experience prompted a theorem: Grades seem to make the most sense when they rest on the least information.

The same principle holds in competency programs. Information about the student is kept to an absolute minimum, so that everyone involved may enjoy the greatest confidence in the results. The decision rests only on a single, special test, while decision makers deliberately close their eyes to a great deal of pertinent information. The school files bulge with several years' worth of grade sheets, test scores, evaluations by teachers and counselors, and examples of students' own work. On the faculty are dozens of experienced adults who can speak with authority, from close personal observation, about the capabilities of any student. Yet when it comes time for certification, this wealth of easily available information plays no part whatsoever. All that counts is the score from a few dozen multiple-choice items, a very sparse indicator indeed. More facts would only confuse the issue.

As an exercise, a kind of thought experiment, let us devise a minimum competency scheme that requires no special test. It ought to draw instead on the store of information and impressions that the school has already gathered about each student. The task: to determine which students are entitled to a diploma, according to minimum competency standards.

Actually, for all but a few students it should not be that difficult. Once or twice during the school year, the teachers might meet for a day or two to read through the list of juniors and seniors not yet certified. Most students ought to pass with very little discussion, just a nod around the table. A few might fail the same way. Only those individuals uncomfortably close to the borderline should require any real debate.

Several objections to the idea come to mind at once. The objections lead to an interesting observation on the use of tests instead of this scheme, so they are worth enumerating: The teachers would make mistakes; the process would take up too much of teachers' time; it would cost too much; there would be no way to maintain a uniformity of standards; teachers' prejudices might bias the results; there could be disagreement among teachers on whether to certify particular students; and there would be no good defense against a failed student who complained.

Giving a test seems to avoid all these problems. It is more correct, though, to say that the test is subject to many of the same objections but hides them under the cloak of supposed objectivity. The problems remain. And the last one listed above may turn out to be the most important: It is much easier for administrators to meet an angry parent with official-looking computer printouts than it is to stand on a collection of teachers' impressions.

Teachers will, of course, make occasional mistakes under the scheme I have described. Any human process is subject to error. But the tests make mistakes, too; far more than most people realize. Even assuming that a test is in full compliance with industry standards, a group of teachers should be able to do at least as well. Moreover, certain students are especially liable to misrepresentation in test scores — the handicapped, for example, and those who speak English as a second language. The teachers at least can see beyond these more obvious impediments, as the test cannot.

Will teacher-made decisions take too much time? A few days of meetings, a few minutes of discussion on each student, seems little enough time for an evaluation that caps twelve full years of schooling and means so much to the student's future. The meetings will incur some added cost in teachers' time. But at graduation, the student will have spent more than 10,000 hours in classrooms. Even allowing for the reversed student-teacher ratio at the meeting — many teachers discussing one student — the expense of a five-minute discussion is a vanishing fraction of what it cost to educate that student. That five minutes will determine the outcome of the 10,000 hours. On any relative basis, the cost is very low.

How great will be the threat to uniform standards? The apparent uniformity in the tests is an illusion, as we have seen. Working from state-provided written guidelines, an informed group of teachers ought to do much better. The group as a whole will serve as a counterweight to any individual teacher with a consistently conservative or liberal eye. And unlike the test, the teachers will be able to interpret the guidelines over a broad range of the student's work — "All right, he got nowhere with *Moby Dick;* but how is he with a ninth-grade textbook?"

Teachers' prejudices are a potential problem, the main reason why one teacher alone must not be trusted with the decision on any student. Tests show prejudice as well, as we have seen — sometimes quite systematically. A group of teachers seeking consensus, however, should be able to dampen most prejudices in its individual members. Still, the possibility of all the teachers being prejudiced in the same direction, remote though it is, suggests the need for some sort of review or reconsideration process to which the student can appeal as a matter of course.

And teachers will sometimes disagree. Excellent! Disagreement suggests a student who does some things better than others, or who works better in certain surroundings than others. Such a student is not likely to emerge clearly at all on a sheet of test scores. Disagreement might also suggest prejudice, one way or the other. These are the students for whom the decision will be the most difficult — and because of that, the most meaningful once made.

Compared to the teacher-conference mechanism, the test does have certain practical advantages. It is quicker, probably cheaper, and administratively easier to handle. It reduces the actual decision making to nothing, simply the comparison of each student's score to the predetermined cutoff. A computer can handle that with no trouble. Use of a test, in fact, makes practically no demands on school personnel's time or judgment.

The test's main advantage, however, may be its mystique of infallibility. Many school people, even those who should know better, feel that they can rest comfortably with test scores. There need be no fretting over tough decisions, no guilt over destroying a student's future through denial of certification. There is a simple reply to parents who feel wronged: "This test is required by the state. Your child failed it. It's not our fault he won't graduate."

The test, in short, offers a simple and effective way for schools to pass the buck. No one need feel responsible to account for a student's failure, except for the student himself. In many cases, the failure is not properly the student's own fault at all. But the test leaves him or her little recourse to object.

The very simplicity of the test is also its most severe shortcoming. In a word, the use of a simple test for so important a purpose dehumanizes the educational process. Judgments that ought to be made by thoughtful people who know the students well are made blindly instead, by mechanical means. The message to the student is clear: All that matters, in the end, is the test score. Good class work, good grades, and effort beyond the minimum will all count for nothing.

The test itself is not the problem; the problem is the all-or-nothing importance that attaches to the results. If the test were a minor formality on the way to graduation, like being measured for a cap and gown, there would be no serious objection to it. A test with no important effects would be at worst an inconvenience.

For a great many students, the test in practice is just such a formality. These are the students placing in the top half or two-thirds of their class—more in some schools, less in others. They have done reasonably well in school all their lives. Most have plans for college. There is no doubt as to their graduation with the proper diploma. The test may indirectly reduce the attention paid to these students, pedagogically. But otherwise, its main immediate effect on them is only a morning wasted in shading little ovals on an answer sheet.

The lower a student stands in the class, however, the less of a formality the test becomes. (For those at the very bottom, it may be a formality of failure.) Only for students near the borderline is the test really important—and for them, the test is so important as to dwarf every other aspect of their education. For the borderline people who fail the few dozen questions, the whole twelve years will have been a total loss. For those who pass, it will all have been worthwhile.

To borderline students especially, the test makes the diploma more important than the education it is supposed to represent. Better students leave school with an education, using the word in its proper, precompetency sense. Students who are certain to fail leave with nothing. But students near the borderline, those for whom passing the test is most in question, will not leave high school as educated people; even the staunchest advocate of competency testing cannot claim that. The test is only for "minimum competency" in a very narrow range of skills. The students who barely pass it carry away at most that minimal set of skills—and the diploma itself.

Between the skills and the diploma, the diploma has by far the greater practical value. The skills are all but useless without the diploma in the employment market. But with a diploma and no skills, one can still make a living of sorts; many high school graduates do, nowadays. The student can only conclude that the diploma is more important than the education it stands for. And it is the competency program, with its threat of no diploma at all, that elevates the diploma to this stature.

Competency programs also put a psychological value on the diploma itself that it may not have had before. Social psychologists have conducted many studies on the question of why certain symbols become desirable. One important factor seems to be the value that other people attach to the symbol, whether or not the symbol itself warrants it. (For example, otherwise ordinary clothing with a designer's name sewn prominently on the outside fetches a premium price. Cigarette smoking is popular among teenagers largely because other teenagers smoke. And so on.) With young children, it is easy to make almost any symbol attractive, simply by convincing them that other children have already found it attractive.

The state does something rather similar. It says, "Henceforth the diploma shall be awarded as a mark of worth," though not much is said about how much worth the diploma really represents. Nevertheless, the borderline student looks around for other marks of social recognition that might apply to him — and finds none. Not surprisingly, the diploma itself becomes his goal.

Even the courts may have fallen into this view. Recall Peter W., the high school graduate who could not read well enough to look for a job. The California courts refused to award him compensation for his lack of an education. Yet in the *Debra P.* opinion, a suit not for an education but for a diploma, Judge Carr was able to write, "[T]he Plaintiffs . . . have a property right in graduation from high school with a standard diploma if they have fulfilled the present requirements for graduation exclusive of the SSAT II requirement."[2] The courts stand ready to protect the symbol, but not what the symbol stands for.

The minimum competency movement set out to make the diploma meaningful. It has succeeded, with a vengeance. The diploma has become not just meaningful, but all-important. As a result, neither the educational establishment nor many of the students it serves can afford any longer to take much of an interest in education. With the goal of minimum competency ordained by law and enforced by the marketplace of employment, all other priorities have to give way before it. In raising the worth of the diploma, minimum competency testing and its diploma sanction inevitably diminish the worth of education.

In spite of this indictment, there are many valuable lessons to be learned from the competency experience. Perhaps the most important — one we must relearn often — is that complex problems rarely yield to simple solutions. A second finding: Simple solutions rarely stay simple for long, if the problems are complex.

All of these are relatively abstract arguments, but there is a stern reality that must be dealt with. In just the past few years, competency testing has become an industry in its own right. It has commercial interests to protect, jobs to safeguard, and a substantial political base. These are always part of any large, ongoing operation. But these interests also give the operation its own reasons for survival, reasons having nothing to do with the original mission. Thus, even if there came a sudden, widespread consensus that competency testing were wrong, it still would not disappear overnight.

When competency testing was first proposed, it impressed many people as a good idea. Who could reasonably object to granting a high school diploma only on the condition that the candidate can read and write? Moreover, the proposal seemed to strike at the core of several problems in education, including the common perception that "frills" had replaced the basics. Along with reestablishing the diploma to its former status, as a mark of real achievement, a simple testing mechanism would encourage both teachers and students to get down to business. As an added bonus, the very same scheme would single out the children who needed extra help, in time for them to get it. Most important of all, however, the next generation would know how to read.

Competency testing seemed like a good idea at the time. (That applies to many innovations in education.) Now, we are far enough along to know that it is not working. We also know why it is not working. In a word, making a test was a poor place to begin solving the problems of education. We tried to adjust the machine by moving the knob that was easiest to reach, and it turned out to be the wrong one.

The competency establishment will resist this news. It has little to fear, though. The operation is already far too big to dismantle. Furthermore, there is still important work to be done that the minimum competence machinery might be able to handle—if it can first set aside its present objectives.

We need a better consensus than we have on the goals of schooling—not rigid regulations, to be sure, but a consensus that leaves plenty of room for local experimentation. The competency movement has begun the process of developing a consensus and has brought it quite far along in terms of skills. Much of this experience ought to be valuable in the future, if addressed to a broader range of goals. There are new lines of communication between the states and the localities within them and new forms of collaboration on educational issues among agencies at different governmental levels. In many states the collaboration is forced by legislative action, but once the channels are open, they can serve purposes far more productive than setting competency standards. Local agencies seem to be talking to one another more, and even the states seem willing to learn from each other's experiences. The federal government too, especially through the National Institute of Education, is learning to provide advice and support with less interference than formerly. These are no small accomplishments. Even if the stricter forms of minimum competency testing do not survive the next few years of court action, some of the processes that the movement has engendered should be encouraged to continue and to grow.

We still need to find the children who are at risk, educationally; we need to find them before their disillusionment sets in. We must learn how to help them promptly and effectively without causing them embarrassment among their peers. Minimum competency has brought a fresh urgency to this very old problem of finding the students who need help, spurred on by the political consequences of withholding diplomas from too many students. The problem was there long before minimum competency testing arrived and will be there long after it expires. The attention the problem receives is very welcome and deserves encouragement of every possible kind.

We also have to develop ways of reaching the students who are now slipping through the educational system's fingers entirely. In the past, we have tried to help them according to category—black, handicapped, Hispanic, deprived, special. That will no longer do. All the words designating these categories were once euphemisms for older, cruder terms, a sure signal of social suspicion covered over with fresh terminology. The unseemly scrambling of ever-smaller minorities for their share of federal funds is further evidence that allocating attention by category misses the point.

The minimum competency movement has the beginnings of a better approach, that of sorting people according to ability, rather than by social group, ethnicity, or diagnosis of handicap. It is a powerful idea and one that was, for many generations, a professed aspiration of American society as a whole. Its time may be returning.

Government agencies, for example, commonly write program regulations that prohibit discrimination on the grounds of race, creed, color, religion, national origin, sex, native language, handicap, and so on in an increasingly unwieldy list. An unknown bureaucrat has finally exercised his admirable gift for brevity: no discrimination in his programs except on the basis of ability. That phrasing would do well to catch on, in view of pending movements for equality on the part of homosexuals, fat people, older people, ugly people, retarded people, pregnant people, and doubtless others too numerous to mention. All of their causes are just. The words "except on the basis of ability" would accommodate every minority at a stroke, except perhaps the incompetent.

The minimum competency movement has something similar in mind — intentional discrimination on the basis of ability. In terms of remediation, funding allocations, and the like, the movement puts the emphasis precisely where it belongs. In the early vision of the competency movement, a student's color or handicap or social status would neither work against him nor gain him special preference. Anyone who could pass the test would receive a diploma; anyone who could not, would not. Other educational tests claim to give the same kind of "equal treatment." But before competency testing, governmental agencies rarely tried to select groups for special treatment solely on the basis of ability.

The movement might have accomplished its goal, if the art of testing were more advanced than it is. However, the idea ran aground on tests that are simply not up to what the competency programs demand of them. The best tests available are still, unfortunately, too sensitive to many characteristics about the test-taker besides his ability, including race, social standing, and handicap. In practice, the ideal of discrimination solely on the grounds of ability continues to elude us. And until we can achieve it, denying people diplomas on the basis of test scores will continue to be unfair. But the underlying philosophy, evaluating by competence rather than social group, is a step in the right direction.

The Need for Political Change

This book has criticized at some length the two main predicates on which the competency movement is built, the test and the diploma sanction, and some of the more specific objectives as well. At the same time, however, the movement has other goals and methods that are worth careful preservation — ideas about collaboration among local and state governments, detection, diagnosis, remediation, and equal treatment. These have the potential for producing badly needed improvements in education, and the competency movement may have developed the machinery to pursue them. The improvements, however, are not likely to come about as long as the present objectives persist. It is a matter of finding that the better mousetrap is not very good at catching mice after all, but that it might make an excellent cheese slicer.

The goals of the competency movement were politically motivated from the start, particularly the stress on basic life skills and the insistence that the diploma become meaningful. The mechanism chosen for achieving the goals also makes more sense politically than it does educationally — i.e., use of a test, instead of more direct intervention in the educational process. Accordingly, the goals and the mechanisms are unlikely to change until the political climate does.

The political change, when it comes, will have to take several forms. One of the most important will be the willingness once again to trust educators with the business of education. The legislatures will still want to effect change, occasionally. It is their prerogative, as elected representatives of the people. But the legislatures can better serve the public will through the people they appoint to run the educational system. A corporation's directors do not take their instructions straight to workers on the assembly line; the result would be chaos. It is equally bad management for the highest authority in a state to enact its demands directly upon the students. When educators then try to save students from the consequences of the enactment, they indeed find themselves carrying out the legislative intent with regard to basic skills. But legislation through a test makes for a poor mechanism of control—too inflexible, too unresponsive to varying conditions—for so complicated an enterprise as education.

A closely related political change will be a disentangling of causes from effects. Minimum competency legislation specifies an effect—a score on a multiple-choice test—and leaves the causes of that score largely to take care of themselves. In certain situations this is a reasonable way to proceed. The government can properly require that new cars average a certain gasoline mileage and let the manufacturers figure out how best to accomplish it. To focus on effects is often the simplest way to operate, politically. It makes good press, and it leads to swift consensus—not just in education, but in many aspects of public life.

The gasoline-mileage issue makes a poor analogy to education, however. In the case of automobiles, other regulations and the forces of the marketplace combine to ensure that new cars are up to snuff in a great many respects, not just gasoline economy. With no such countervailing forces in education—there is less regulation and the clientele is captive—the emphasis on effects has produced distortion in the causes. It is as if we had only one car manufacturer and the government regulated its gas mileage and little else. The result, no doubt, would be a slow, uncomfortable, unexciting, unsafe automobile that got great gas mileage. In much the same way, the educational system is now on the way to subordinating all else to competency test scores. Education too is in danger of becoming slow, uncomfortable, unexciting, and—in terms of larger national goals—quite unsafe.

Another kind of political change will have to be renewed respect for the diversity of people who inhabit the United States. In other areas of public concern, we do see a refreshing openness to hitherto unrecognized minorities; examples range all the way from wheelchair ramps and closed-caption television programs to maternity clothes obviously meant for pregnant lawyers and business executives.

In education, however, the attention to minorities has been more heavy-handed and less accepting. The style tends toward isolated programs for one minority at a time, reaching ever-smaller groups as the years and the Congresses go by. And the goal in each case seems to be homogenization with the American mean. To be sure, the mean no longer looks as white, suburban, and middle-class as it used to, as evidenced by the appearance in children's textbooks first of blacks, then Hispanics, and now handicapped youngsters. But the outcome sought, for each newly recognized minority, remains basically the middle-class, English-speaking values with a sprinkling of cultural self-respect for flavor.

Depending on a child's aspirations and potential, this kind of education may or may not be necessary. While it is essential for a student who hopes some day to take on a position of influence and leadership in the larger society, this kind of education presents two types of problems for many minority students. First, setting the white, middle-class, English-speaking image as the goal rigs the game heavily against minority children from the start. It puts them at an enormous competitive disadvantage, because white, middle-class, English-speaking children have less to learn to do as well. Second, the need to fit an unfamiliar mold makes it less likely that minority students will find the motivation to finish their education at all, and in fact, the dropout rate among most minorities is far higher than among their white Anglo counterparts.

This question of dominant values is not peculiar to education; it merely reflects our mechanisms for allocating power throughout society as a whole. The people among us who have the most influence are, in large majority, white male Protestants who speak excellent English. Some minority people sense a conspiracy to keep them out of power, but the truth may be less maleficent — something as simple as the people in charge feeling most comfortable among others like themselves (as we all do) and so tending to choose people like themselves for their successors. With either explanation, a teacher who hopes to see his students succeed will try to help them resemble people who have succeeded already. Therein, I suspect, is the cause for the furor among teachers and black parents alike over a court decision that upheld the use of black English as a teaching device in the schools.

Education has come a long way toward recognizing minorities but is not yet willing to accord their cultures and ways of life the same respect as it gives to majority values. To expect that of the schools would be futile, as long as discrimination remains so pervasive in other institutions. Yet the cost of seeking to remold minority children runs extremely high; against those who do succeed in white society must be balanced the millions more who, finding school intolerable, turn to the street instead. There is no easy solution to a problem rooted as deeply as this one. Regardless of how they approach it, whether they try to serve the future or the present, the schools are certain to let down a large number of minority children.

There would be no such problem in a society that truly accepted diversity among its members. Conversely, without such acceptance, the problem is bound to persist. It is reasonable to ask, though, that the legislatures refrain from aggravating it.

Minimum competency enacts into law, albeit in a muted way, the philosophy that a certain kind and amount of education is correct for everyone. The legislation stems explicitly from the notion that no person can succeed, again in a limited sense, without that minimum. It is quite a piece of effrontery, if one stops to think about it, to maintain that these skills, and no others, are what a person absolutely requires to make his way in the world.

The prescription will turn out to be right for some people. No doubt others could manage to lead reasonably productive lives without knowing how to figure unit prices and sales tax — if lack of a diploma did not bar them from all meaningful employment. And for still others, the standards are so low as to set up a parody of what their education ought to be.

It offends both reason and common sense to suppose that any one set of standards can possibly make sense for every student in a state. To describe the standard as a "minimum" does not relieve the absurdity; it merely penalizes the student who fails to meet it. The proposition of a single standard overlooks the tremendous range of capabilities among students; it puts excessive demands on some and lets most off far too easily. And it ignores the diversity of work force that our economy can accommodate. Requirements for jobs cover a vast spectrum of academic skills and abilities, ranging from those demanding many years of post-graduate training to mostly manual occupations best learned on the job. No single cutoff point, no matter where it is placed, can reasonably apply to everyone.

As it happens, most of the states have chosen a cutoff point that passes almost all of the white English-speaking students. A heavily disproportionate number of the failures are minority people. Again, one can look to a conspiracy theory; or it may be that political considerations dictate a cutoff score that passes a certain number of students overall, with minority failure an unintended result. Bias in the test, and discrimination in the education that precedes it, may also be significant factors.

Whether intentionally or not, the competency mechanism discriminates against several minorities. But given the nature of the scheme, some kind of discrimination is almost inevitable. The skills tested are those long considered important by the majority culture, and in which most white English-speaking students have generations of experience. A lot of minority children start with a relative background disadvantage with respect to these particular skills. Then, the imposition of a uniform standard on a highly nonuniform student body assures an uneven distribution of results, escalating the minority disadvantage to a matter of permanent record. Finally, the diploma sanction makes the student's failure to reach the standard publicly visible, denies him most worthwhile employment, and thereby threatens to carry over the inequality into the next generation.

The core of the problem, once again, is the notion that a single standard will do for everyone. Such rigid uniformity is neither essential to the economy nor desirable in its social consequences. In view of the limited motivations behind it, primarily the award of credentials and the redress of priorities in education, the imposition of a single standard does far more harm than good.

The Need for Excellence

Minimum competency testing also has other, more serious consequences that may not take effect for another generation or two — consequences stemming from the impact of a single standard on the pursuit of excellence in our schools.

To some educators nowadays, excellence is rapidly becoming a frill, rather like new band uniforms. No point in worrying about excellence, they say, until the kids can read and write. First things first.

Such a view is disastrously shortsighted. For one thing, most of the kids can read and write perfectly well and need the encouragement to strive for more. For another — and this is not a welcome thought in these populist times, but a fact nonetheless — much of lasting human achievement has come from a small fraction of the population who have sought improvement. In medicine, athletics, science, music, engineering, and every other field, these are the people who strove for excellence. Some of them accomplished it, and the rest of us have benefited immeasurably from their efforts.

It sounds naive to express such ideas in a generation that has come to question the value of much recent progress. But still, it is hard to fault the virtual eradication of smallpox from the earth, or indoor plumbing, or the Brandenburg Concertos. And regardless of one's views on the social costs of progress, it is only the continuing quest for improvement in the quality of life that keeps us today from hunkering in the cave over a haunch of raw meat.

The need to try for excellence is part of being human. It takes many forms, some more productive than others. A poet, a businessman, a rock musician, and an arsonist might each seek to excel in what they do — to produce, for once, the perfect piece of work. Or, each might be content merely to go through the motions and settle for the ordinary. But almost everyone would like to excel in something. It need not be in work; it need not be something that will change the world. Some people seek to be superb at bowling or dancing or telling jokes or knowing the best places to buy clothes. It is all part of the same drive. Seeing some of its expressions is enough to give one pride in the species.

The quest to excel predates formal schooling by a good many millenia. There must have once been a family dissatisfied with tilling the field by hand and willing to think about alternatives. Somehow the family managed to domesticate an ox, or perhaps it was a buffalo, and thereby gained both motive power for cultivation and a self-propelled food supply. By any standards, it was an excellent achievement. But that rarely happens any more. For the past few centuries at least, humankind's most valuable accomplishments have come from people whose work rested on a formal education. It is hard to imagine an unlettered individual developing the polio vaccine or inventing the truck-borne freezers that safely distribute perishable food.

Apart from providing the knowledge on which people can build, school is a major force in directing the child's need to excel. Some students, convinced that school is the enemy, become experts at vandalism or at terrorizing fellow students. Some direct their energies outside school altogether; with occasional exceptions, their accomplishments do little to benefit either society or themselves. And some try to satisfy the need to excel within the large range of opportunities that the modern school makes available, whether in academic subjects like science or literature, or in other activities like drama, art, athletics, or music.

This last group are the people most likely to make a mark on the world. Equally important, they may also be the ones most likely to live fully satisfying lives. I know a man whose distinction lies in knowing by heart all of the baseball records from 1892 to the present. No doubt this accomplishment brings him pleasure and respect from his friends; otherwise he would not have gone to the trouble. Another acquaintance takes pride in knowing the names of all the minor actors on television. Nearly all of us, it seems, have some achievement to call our own. Nevertheless, and though value judgments on this sort of thing are probably unwise, it seems reasonable that people whose interests are less restricted, whose searches span broader and richer terrains, can take more pleasure in the hunt—in tracking the spoor of new ideas—and, when the prey is come upon at last, in the kill.

There is special fulfillment for those whose quest brings them achievements warranting attention from a large public. And some individuals in every generation find the satisfaction of knowing that they have made the lives of others a little easier, or a little more enjoyable. Some years ago, a man of my acquaintance invented a device that enables radio stations to broadcast music with less distortion than before. It was a minor step in electronics, and it made him very little money. Yet he takes great pride in the pleasure that his gadget now brings to music lovers all over this country and Europe, even though only a handful are aware of either him or his invention. Again with rare exceptions, most out-of-school pursuits simply cannot provide that kind of reward, let alone the fame and money that sometimes come with it.

An even more important reward is merely the search for excellence itself. The mark of the true artist or craftsman is his striving to meet his own standards, which he raises each time he attains them. Over such a person's lifetime, as over the span of human history, dissatisfaction with the past is often the key to excellence in the future. This too sounds like heresy, in an era that looks back longingly to the past while it devises new expensive therapies to teach people to be satisfied with their present selves. But the push to do things better, to seek one's own form of excellence among the bewildering variety of possibilities, goes on around us unabated, nonetheless.

Until quite recently, the schools considered exhortation toward excellence part of their job. The departure seems to have begun in the 1950s with the spread of a philosophy that played down competition among students, stressing instead the intrinsic and equal worth of every child. But at least through the mid-1960s, there was still plenty of attention to students with the motivation to do good work. That was, in many ways, an exciting time in education, marked by earnest searches for improvement at all levels. It was perhaps most apparent in the sciences, where the post-Sputnik educational reforms were in full swing. And in other subject areas as well, students who excelled received a great deal of encouragement for further study.

At the time when the minimum competency movement appeared, however, it had become quite unfashionable to praise those who were successful, lest their not-so-capable classmates take offense. The trend has at least four causes — or possibly effects; it is hard to tell here which is which.

One factor is social promotion, the practice of moving students along with their age-mates regardless of how prepared they are to undertake the work in the next grade. A second is grade inflation, under which most students now receive Bs and often As for work of no special merit. (One piece of evidence is the ascending grade averages nationwide in the face of declining test scores; in some schools, a C is tantamount to failure.) The third cause (or effect) was an earlier trend away from rigorous academic courses in high schools and toward more and softer electives — in other words, a lessening of demands on students. These three factors, incidentally, are often cited among the reasons for installing competency testing programs. And they all undercut motivation to do excellent work.

A fourth factor, by far the most sensitive politically, has been educators' reluctance to maintain visible evaluation systems that sometimes gave a poor accounting of minority students. This reluctance also arose in the mid-1960s, the time of the Great Society, when the federal government began putting billions of dollars into "closing the gap" between minority and white/Anglo students. Pressure soon mounted on the schools to show positive results — or at least, to make negative results less conspicuous. The social scientists joined in, arguing that public distinctions of students' performance were often destructive to minority children's self-esteem and so impaired their performance. By the early 1970s, the situation had become so discouraging that some Washington officials quietly wondered if the only way to close the gap would be somehow to hold back the white students. There is no evidence that such a plan was ever actually attempted. But the depth of frustration that it represents is certainly consistent with the movement, then reaching its peak, of downplaying comparisons among students altogether.

All four of these factors — social promotions, grade inflation, relaxation of course requirements, and minority concerns — made it harder to tell which students were doing well and which were doing badly. That was precisely one of the goals behind these trends—to avoid singling out the students at the bottom. Unfortunately, the same measures made it just as difficult to identify students at the top, those doing exceptionally good work. Not only was high achievement made less conspicuous to the public, but the students themselves, all receiving much the same grades and recognition, had no way of telling whether extra effort was paying off. More exactly, it was clear to many students that extra effort did *not* pay off—that a bright student's grade transcripts would look just about the same whether he loafed his way through school or did his best.

It is a demoralizing situation, hardly one calculated to draw out someone's greatest efforts. A few students no doubt have the inner drive to do good work anyway. But there are many distractions in the teenage years, and the message from the schools could not be clearer: Adequate work is all you need to look successful; good work will not pay off; the effort needed for excellent work will be a waste of time.

Minimum competency testing is a further impediment to the pursuit of excellence. Some of the reasons have appeared elsewhere in this book, including trivialization of curriculum and the shifting of resources away from good students. But even more important may be the social policy that minimum competency testing brings with it, at least in the eyes of our more capable young people.

Among poor students, the competency programs intentionally undo the effects of the four factors listed above; they seek precisely to single out the students at the bottom. But the competency tests and their reporting systems make no distinctions above that very low minimum. The tests treat all students who pass as equivalent. This one distinction of minimalcy is often the only public evaluation available, the only visible dividing line that reflects the quality of students' work. The test functions like an optical illusion; the imposition of a very sharp, very bright boundary makes it that much harder to distinguish the already faint shades of gray around it. The four factors continue to obscure the differences among students in the middle range and above. People with the potential to excel thus have all the more reason not to bother; they will just be lumped with all the other test-passers anyway.

The legislatures send a message with the competency tests: This is the least we expect of you. A second message comes from the school: We neither know nor care who does exceptionally well. The combination is devastating; it says that passing the competency tests is *all* that society expects. Good work takes a lot of time and real effort. Why should anyone bother?

Of all the charges raised against competency testing here and elsewhere, this is the most serious. Excellence is a scarce commodity in the best of times. We simply cannot afford to waste it. Not to encourage excellence is bad enough, but actively to turn it aside is unspeakable. That was not the intent behind minimum competency testing but nonetheless is one of its overriding effects.

Even if every other aspect of the competency programs were working beneficially, this alone would be ample reason to end the movement. Minimum competency testing deliberately lets fall the bottom few percent of the student population. Apparently their loss was reckoned as part of the cost — presumably an acceptable sacrifice to improved education. But the testing program also drops, just as surely, the top few percent of students as well. That is a sacrifice no society can make. It sets the cost impossibly high — not just for us, but also for the generations to come.

Notes

1. This remark is not quite true as it stands. The mathematical unit of information is the "bit," which is the amount of information carried by a yes/no message when both are equally probable. The information delivered by the flip of a coin amounts to precisely one bit. But if one outcome is less probable than the other, then it carries more information when it happens. In a sense, information is a measure of surprise. That a particular student has passed his competency exam, when most students are expected to pass, is a fact that carries very little information, mathematically speaking.

2. 474 F. Supp. 244, 266 (citations omitted).

References

Airasian, P. W. 1979. What are the educational implications of minimum competency? *National Elementary Principal* 58 (January): 35–37.

Anderson, B. D. 1977. *The costs of legislated minimal competency requirements.* Prepared with the assistance of a contract from the National Institute of Education. St. Louis: Washington University.

Baratz, J. C. 1979. What are the social implications of minimum competency? *National Elementary Principal* 58 (January): 38–40.

Beckham, J. 1980. *Legal implications of minimum competency testing.* Fastback no. 138. Bloomington, Ind.: Phi Delta Kappa Educational Foundation.

Block, J. H., and Burns, R. B. 1976. Mastery learning. In *Review of Research in Education,* vol. 4, ed. L. S. Schulman, pp. 3–49. Itasca, Ill.: F. E. Peacock.

Brandwein, P. F-. 1971. *The permanent agenda of man: the humanities.* New York: Harcourt Brace Jovanovich.

Bricknell, H. M. 1978. Seven key notes on minimum competency testing. In *A citizens' introduction to minimum competency programs for students,* pp. 25–34. Columbia, S.C.: Southeastern Public Education Program.

Buros, O. K. 1977. Fifty years in testing: some reminiscences, criticisms, and suggestions. *Educational Researcher* 6 (July/August): 9–15.

Callahan, R. E. 1962. *Education and the cult of efficiency.* Chicago: University of Chicago Press.

College Entrance Examination Board. 1977. *On further examination: report of the advisory panel on the scholastic aptitude test score decline.* Princeton.

Corbett, W. D. 1979. What principals can do about the secrecy issue. *National Elementary Principal* 58 (January): 58–59.

Cronbach, L. J. 1970. *Essentials of psychological testing.* 3d ed. New York: Harper & Row.

———. 1975. Five decades of public controversy over mental testing. *American Psychologist* 30 (January): 1–14.

Davis, R. B. 1974. New math: success/failure? *Education Digest* 39 (March): 11–13.

Dearman, N. B., and Plisko, V. W. 1979. *The condition of education.* National Center for Education Statistics. Washington, D.C.: U.S. Government Printing Office.

———. 1980. *The condition of education.* National Center for Education Statistics. Washington, D.C.: U.S. Government Printing Office.

Education Daily. May 27, 1980. Judge bars Florida schools from using competency tests.

Frahm, R., and Covington, J. 1979. *What's happening in minimum competency testing.* Bloomington, Ind.: Phi Delta Kappa.

Glickman, C. D. 1979. Mastery learning stifles individuality. *Educational Leadership* 37 (November): 100–102.

Gorth, W. P., and Perkins, M. R. 1979. *A study of minimum competency testing programs: final summary and analysis report.* Amherst, Mass.: National Evaluation Systems.

Haney, W., and Madaus, G. 1978*a*. Making sense of the competency testing movement. *Harvard Educational Review* 48: 462–484.

———. 1978*b*. *National consortium on testing: staff circular no. 2.* Cambridge, Mass.: Huron Institute.

———. 1979*a*. What are the educational implications of minimum competency? *National Elementary Principal* 58 (January): 32–34.

———. 1979*b*. What can minimum competency accomplish? *National Elementary Principal* 58 (January): 25–28.

———. 1979*c*. Why minimum competency now? *National Elementary Principal* 58 (January): 15–18.

Hoffmann, B. 1962. *The tyranny of testing.* New York: Collier Books.

Houts, P. L., ed. 1977. *The myth of measurability.* New York: Hart.

———. 1979. The Wingspread papers: a report on the minimum competency movement. *National Elementary Principal* 58 (January): 12–14.

Hyman, J. S., and Cohen, S. A. 1979. Learning for mastery: ten conclusions after 15 years and 3,000 schools. *Educational Leadership* 37 (November): 104–109.

Jencks, C. 1978. What's behind the drop in test scores? *Working Papers For a New Society* 6 (July/August): 29–41.

Jencks, C., et al. 1972. *Inequality: a reassessment of the effect of family and schooling in America.* New York: Basic Books.

Jensen, A. R. 1969. How much can we boost IQ and scholastic achievement? *Harvard Educational Review* 39: 1–123.

Kohn, S. D. 1979. Digging at the roots of the minimum competency movement. *National Elementary Principal* 58 (January): 42–47.

Lazarus, M. 1974*a*. Toward a new program in mathematics. *National Elementary Principal* 53 (January/February): 72–81.

———. 1974*b*. Mathophobia: some personal speculations. *National Elementary Principal* 53 (January/February): 16–22.

———. 1975. Rx for mathophobia. *Saturday Review* (November): 46.

———. 1977*a*. Coming to terms with testing. In *The myth of measurability,* ed. P. L. Houts, pp. 183–196. New York: Hart.

———. 1977*b*. On the misuse of test data: a second look at Jencks's *Inequal-*

ity. In *The myth of measurability,* ed. P. L. Houts, pp. 324–330. New York: Hart.

_____. 1978. Reckoning with calculators. *National Elementary Principal* 57 (January): 71–77.

_____. 1980*a.* Courts frown on teaching at home. *Education USA* 22 (March): 220.

_____. 1980*b.* PL 94-142 and the courts—so far. *Education USA* 22 (May): 276–277.

Levine, M. 1976. The academic achievement test: its historical context and social functions. *American Psychologist* 31 (March): 228–238.

Lyman, H. B. 1978. *Test scores and what they mean.* 3d ed. Englewood Cliffs, N.J.: Prentice-Hall.

McClung, M. S. 1977. Competency testing: potential for discrimination. *Clearinghouse Review* (September): 439–448.

_____. 1978. Are competency testing programs fair? legal? *Phi Delta Kappan* 59 (February): 397–400.

_____. 1979. *Footnotes* (November). Denver: Education Commission of the States.

_____. 1980. *Footnotes* (February). Denver: Education Commission of the States.

McClung, M. S., and Pullin, D. 1978. Competency testing and handicapped students. *Clearinghouse Review* (March): 922–927.

Miller, B. S., ed. 1978. *Minimum competency testing: a report of four regional conferences.* St. Louis: Cemrel.

National Council of Supervisors of Mathematics. 1976. *Position paper on basic mathematical skills.* Report prepared pursuant to a contract with the National Institute of Education, U.S. Department of Health, Education, and Welfare. Minneapolis.

National Council of Teachers of Mathematics. 1980. *An agenda for action: recommendations for school mathematics of the 1980s.* Reston, Va.

National School Public Relations Association. 1978. *The competency challenge: what schools are doing.* Arlington, Va.

Pipho, C. 1979*a.* Competency testing: a response to Arthur Wise. *Educational Leadership* 36 (May): 551–554.

_____. 1979*b.* *Update VIII: minimum competency testing.* Denver: Education Commission of the States.

Schwartz, J. L. 1977*a.* A is to B as C is to anything at all: the illogic of IQ tests. In *The myth of measurability,* ed. P. L. Houts, pp. 90–99. New York: Hart.

_____. 1977*b.* Math tests. In *The myth of measurability,* ed. P. L. Houts, pp. 282–290. New York: Hart.

Sells, L. W. 1978. Mathematics—a critical filter. *Science Teacher* 45 (February): 28–29.

Southeastern Public Education Program. 1978. *A citizens' introduction to minimum competency programs for students.* Columbia, S.C.

Suydam, M. N. 1976. *Electronic hand calculators: the implications for pre-*

college education, final report. U.S. Department of Health, Education, and Welfare and the National Science Foundation. Columbus: Ohio State University.

Taylor, E. F. 1977*a*. The looking-glass world of testing. *Today's Education* 66 (March/April): 39–44.

_____. 1977*b*. Science tests. In *The myth of measurability,* ed. P. L. Houts, pp. 291–308. New York: Hart.

Taylor, E. F., and Schwartz, J. L. 1977. A due process procedure for testing. In *The myth of measurability,* ed. P. L. Houts, pp. 346–347. New York: Hart.

Tobias, S. 1975. Math anxiety. *Ms* (September): 56.

_____. 1980. *Overcoming math anxiety.* Boston: Houghton Mifflin.

Tyler, R. W. 1979*a*. What are the educational implications of minimum competency? *National Elementary Principal* 58 (January): 29–31.

_____. 1979*b*. What can minimum competency accomplish? *National Elementary Principal* 58 (January): 28.

Weber, G. 1974. *Uses and abuses of standardized testing in the schools.* Washington, D.C.: Council for Basic Education.

Zacharias, J. R. 1974. The importance of quantitative thinking. *National Elementary Principal* 53 (January/February): 8–13.

_____. 1977. The trouble with IQ tests. In *The myth of measurability,* ed. P. L. Houts, pp. 66–81. New York: Hart.

Zakariya, S. B. 1979. Minimum constitutionality. *National Elementary Principal* 58 (January): 10.

Index